THE HAITIAN MEDIA SYSTEM AND ITS MAIN CHARACTERISTICS

CHARACTERISTICS

TOWARD A NEW THEORETICAL MODEL

THE HAITIAN MEDIA SYSTEM

AND ITS MAIN CHARACTERISTICS

TOWARD A NEW THEORETICAL MODEL

WISNIQUE PANIER

COMMON GROUND

First published in 2023
as part of the *Communication and Media Studies Book Imprint*
doi: 10.18848/978-1-957792-17-0/CGP (Full Book)

Common Ground Research Networks
2001 South First Street, Suite 202
University of Illinois Research Park
Champaign, IL
61820

Library of Congress Cataloging-in-Publication Data

Names: Panier, Wisnique, author.
Title: The Haitian Media System and its Main Characteristics: Toward a New
   Theoretical Model / Wisnique Panier.
Description: Champaign : Common Ground Research Networks, 2023. | Includes
   bibliographical references. | Summary: "After carefully analyzing
   different models of media systems existing in the scientific literature,
   including the three models proposed by Halin and Mancini (2004), the
   author concludes that none of them applies to the Haitian case. In this
   perspective, he presents a new theoretical model of a media system
   called: the model of the precarious system of democratic transition. It
   is based on a dozen fundamental parameters that characterize the Haitian
   media system and the environment in which it operates. This is a
   significant contribution to advancing knowledge in media studies and
   public communication in general. His study confirms the limitations of
   media system models resulting from Halin and Mancini's comparative
   studies of the media systems of 18 Western countries. This book is a
   real reference document that gives a reading grid to analyze the media
   systems of non-Western countries, particularly African or Latin American
   countries, which have characteristics similar to that of Haiti"--
   Provided by publisher.
Identifiers: LCCN 2022055860 (print) | LCCN 2022055861 (ebook) | ISBN
   9781957792187 (hardback) | ISBN 9781957792194 (paperback) | ISBN
   9781957792170 (pdf)
Subjects: LCSH: Mass media--Haiti. | Mass media--Philosophy.
Classification: LCC PN4748.H3 P73 2023 (print) | LCC PN4748.H3 (ebook) |
   DDC 302.23097294--dc23/eng/20230103
LC record available at https://lccn.loc.gov/2022055860
LC ebook record available at https://lccn.loc.gov/2022055861

DEDICATION

This book is dedicated to the actors of the Haitian media system. It is particularly dedicated to the memory of an icon of the Haitian press, Anthony Pascal (KONPÈ FILO), one of the participants in our study, who died on July 31, 2020.

BIOGRAPHY

Wisnique Panier is Minister Counselor at the Permanent Mission of Haiti to the United Nations in New York. He holds a PhD in Public Communication from the Department of Information and Communication of the Faculty of Letters of Laval University (Quebec). His research focuses on the transformation of the Haitian radio system, particularly on changes in the relations between the actors of the system. He is also interested in the attachment of Haitians in the diaspora to the media of their country of origin. He is a founding member and director of the Center for Interdisciplinary Studies on Haitian Media (CEIMH) and a member of several t organization at Université Laval, including the Université Laval Research Commission, Groupe de recherche sur les mutations du journalism—*Research Group on Changes in journalism*—(GRMJ) led by its research director Jean Charron, the Canada Research Chair on Global Migration Dynamics and the ÉDIQ. He is the author of several scientific publications and books.

TABLE OF CONTENTS

List of Abbreviations   *XIII*

Acknowledgements   *XV*

Foreword   *XIX*

Preface   *XXI*

Introduction   1

Historical Overview of the Haitian Media Landscape   9

The Characteristics of the Haitian Media System and its Environment   21

The Factors Explaining the Transformation of the Haitian Media System   37

The Concept of System and Its Properties   41

Comparative Studies of Hallin and Mancini's Media Systems   73

The Contribution of the Haitian Case of Studies on Media Systems   91

Postface   *99*

Bibliography   *103*

LIST OF ABBREVIATIONS

AEAUL: West Indian Students Association of Laval University

AHQ: Haitian Association of Quebec

AJH: Association of Haitian Journalists

AMI: Independent Media Association

ANMH: National Association of Haitian Media

WB: World Bank

CEIMH: Center for Interdisciplinary Studies on Haitian Media

CERUL: Laval University Research Ethics Committee

CONATEL: National Telecommunications Council

IMF: International Monetary Fund

IFRB: International Frequency Registration Committee

IHSI: Haitian Institute of Statistics and Informatics

MCC: Ministry of Culture and Communication

MINUSTAH: United Nations Stabilization Mission in Haiti

MTPC: Ministry of Public Works and Communication

ILO: International Labor Organization

OMRH: Office of Management and Human Resources

NGO: Non-governmental organization:

CEO: Owner Director General

RTNH: Radio and National Television of Haiti

RTVC: Radio and Television Caribbean

SNTPH: National Union of Haitian Press Workers

TNH: National Television of Haiti

TH: Télé-Haïti

TPTC: Public Works Transport and Communication

UNESCO: International Educational and Cultural Organization

VSN: National Security Volunteers.

ACKNOWLEDGEMENTS

This work is far from being an individual work, because it results from my doctoral thesis which involves the participation of an invaluable number of people legal and naturalized status. Listing the latter could prove to be as difficult an exercise as carrying out this study itself, the list would be too long. But there are some names that cannot be mentioned without minimizing the considerable contribution of those whose names do not appear here.

First, I would like to thank the great architect of the universe who kindly wanted me to carry out this study despite the difficulties encountered. Without the infallible support of an exceptional research supervisor, I would not have been able to carry out this study despite my will and determination. Jean Charron is for me more than a research director or a scientific guide. He also is for me a friend, a father, and a mentor to whom I never hesitate to share my personal or family problems outside of our director or professor/student relationship.

Reconciling study, family, and work is not always easy, something which Professor Charron understood very well. His academic rigor, his positive attitude, his spirit of openness, and his wise and always well-founded guidelines make him the best research director I could have ever imagined. Each of his remarks and directives made me aware of my shortcomings and how much I had to and must work ever harder to catch up, to be up to the high level of a PhD student. Each time I leave his office, I see more and more clearly the path of my thesis, with my head filled with good ideas. There has never been a misunderstanding between us that could lead to any deterioration of our relationship.

I would also like to express my deep gratitude to the other members of my thesis committee, Henri Assogba and Danielle Bélanger, who is also my co-supervisor. Their advice, recommendations, and scientific orientations have allowed me to see more clearly and to move forward with confidence in my journey according to their fields of competence.

I thank in a special way the director of the doctoral program, Professor François Demers whom some students call "Mr. Cool," which I could translate into Haitian language as a good man, a good and generous man who cares about his students. His advice, his great understanding, his ability to find practical solutions to the problems of students, especially foreigners, are infallible. I am very grateful to Professor Thiery Watine, who began to guide my steps on the path of research throughout the period of my preparatory schooling. I thank all the professors who have contributed in one way or another to the success of this study. I am thinking of the director of the department, Mrs. Véronique Nguyên-Duy, June Marchand, Manon Niquette, Florence Piron, Guillaume Laztko Toch, Lyne Perón, and Pénélope Daignault.

Without the financial support of the Knowledge and Freedom Foundation (FOCAL), the Open Society Foundation (OSF) and the Ministry of National Education and Vocational Training, I would not have been able to carry out this study. I would also like to thank Université Laval for the additional tuition exemption scholarship and the pathway scholarships. My thanks also go to the Groupe de recherche sur les mutations du journalism (GRMJ), of which I am very proud to be a member, for its financial support. I give my heartfelt thanks to all the participants who answered my questions as part of my empirical data collection activities, whose names remain confidential for ethical reasons. I thank the media bosses who welcomed me for observation days in their media environments. I want to talk specifically about Patrick Moussignac, CEO of Caraïbes FM, Mario Viau, CEO of Signal FM, and Gary Pierre Paul Charles, CEO of Scoop FM.

I thank my family members who have always supported me during this study. Without the presence and support of my wife, Sherline, and the love of my two children, Witshelle and Leo Smith, I would not have enough courage and energy to do this important work. I extend my sincere thanks to my parents, Pierre Vilcera and Marie Madeleine Panier, who never spared their efforts for the education of their children. They are exceptional parents. My thanks also go to my brothers and sisters for their moral support and encouragement. Finally, I would like to thank my friends, my doctoral colleagues in the Department of Information and Communication, whose remarks and suggestions have helped to advance my work.

I especially thank my friend, Féro Dessources, production manager at Signal FM since its creation and with whom I had very long and constructive discussions on the transformation of the Haitian media system. I would also like to thank Engineer Fritz F. Joassin, a broadcasting specialist in Haiti who allowed me to find the list of all the directors of CONATEL since its creation to date. A very special thank you to my former working colleague at Signal FM and friend (Jean-Paul 2022) who contributed significantly to the realization of this thesis.

This passionate about broadcasting radio in Haiti has always been available twenty-four hours a day to exchange ideas with me and provide me with all information deemed necessary for my thesis. I thank all the members of the Center for Interdisciplinary Studies on Haitian Media (CEIMH), especially Jobnel Pierre, Phares Jérôme, and Thomas Hervé Nkoudou for their contribution. A special thank you to my friend Dorcé Ricarson who carefully reread some sections of my thesis and shared with me some very relevant remarks. Thank you to my friend Wilfrid Azarre for many fruitful discussions we had about our respective research work, particularly on methodological issues. Special thanks to those whose names are not on this list, especially our eighty-five respondents. Without their valuable input, this study would not have taken place. A special tribute to the memory of the late Anthony Pascal, known as Conpè Filo, an icon, a hero of the Haitian press who kindly shared his experiences with us through an interview lasting more than two hours. He passed away on July 31, year? but through this study, his experiments will continue to serve the scientific community and the public.

FOREWORD

From an early age, I have always had a great passion for the media world. Journalism has always been my profession of choice. I constantly knew that I was going to spend my entire career in this field, but the precarious conditions in which Haitian journalists work as well as other personal ambitions pushed me to make other professional choices. Nevertheless, despite my advanced studies in the field of law and information and communication sciences, I still feel part of the media world. I often wonder if I should go back to work and make a career as a journalist or if I should find another way to stay in the Haitian media world without continuing in the practice of journalism. The answer took time to come, but it was by observing the evolution of the Haitian media system and noting the almost total absence of scientific studies on Haitian media that I found a way. I told myself that the best way for me to stay in the media field is to contribute to advancing knowledge in this field by capitalizing on the specificities of the Haitian media system, particularly radio, which is the dominant media in Haiti. As is happening in every country in the world, the Haitian media system continues to transform under the influence of several factors, but it remains an almost virgin terrain to explore. A career as a researcher is also for me an even more demanding priesthood than the exercise of journalism itself.

On an axiological and ethical level, I admit that I am working on a reality, the relationships maintained by the actors of the Haitian media system, which I know well, because I have already played the role of several actors in the radio system. First, I worked for more than six years as a journalist. Then, I worked for more than three years as an institutional communications officer and as a press relations officer. This put me in the position of the sources of information. And finally, I am a very savvy listener of various Haitian radio programs. Somewhere my work experiences in the field of journalism contribute to the enrichment of my research work. Nevertheless, I make sure that my personal values and experiences do not influence the process of my research even though the collective values of Haitian society can have great influences on my work.

On the ontological level, the distinct local realities that I observe in the functioning of the Haitian radio system can be understood as a co-construction of the different actors of the system. What I observe is not an immutable reality. It is a discursive construction that results from the relations between the actors of the Haitian radio system. This puts me in a rather constructivist epistemological posture. As Mucchielli (2004) recalls, constructivism as an epistemological positioning bases knowledge and its conditions of elaboration on seven postulates according to which scientific knowledge is at the same time, "constructed; unfinished, plausible, suitable and contingent; goal-oriented; dependent on actions and experiences; made by subjects who know; structured by the process of knowledge while also structuring it; forged in and through the interaction of the knowing subject with the world" (Mucchielli, 2004, 10). This epistemological posture requires field investigations, as is the case in this study. It is based on fundamentally qualitative methodological processes.

Methodologically, the question that arises is how to know or apprehend the media reality that I observe, the transformation of relations between the actors of the Haitian radio system. Thus, I believe that knowledge can be acquired or generated by means of a plurality of methodological approaches, but I opted in this study for a qualitative approach. That is why I use qualitative tools to examine the explanatory factors of the transformation of the different aspects of the Haitian radio system.

PREFACE

The Haitian model, or the model of the precarious system of democratic transition, is entering the scientific world. This theoretical proposal by Wisnique Panier has just shown or confirmed the limits of different models of media system existing in the scientific literature, elaborated based on the characteristics specific to the functioning of the media of Western countries.

The scientific dimension of this book, which you are about to discover, is well established. Because a summary of its content was recently published by the world-renowned scientific journal "Journal of communication and media studies" after successfully undergoing a rigorous double-blind validation process. This book details the theoretical proposal of the author according to about twenty parameters that characterize the functioning of the Haitian media and the environment in which they evolve, as summarized in the last chapter (6) of this book.

Haiti, in recent decades, has experienced a spectacular development in terms of media. The number of radios on the FM band has exploded to the point that it is becoming extremely difficult, if not impossible, to have access to a frequency. It is now a privilege reserved for the wealthy or those close to the political powers. Haiti is perhaps the country with the highest number of radio stations per capita. Online media has been following this trend for some time. The availability of the Internet, the arrival of social networks and the breakthrough of mobile phones in the country favor the development of this type of media that requires little cost for its creation or even maintenance.

While radio has remained the preserve of the powerful and the rich, online media are in most cases owned by journalists. Television is also experiencing some development, but less than radio and the online press. As for the written press—the print version—is recalcitrant to the change that is taking place in the Haitian media field. The country has only two daily newspapers—Le Nouvelliste and Le National—struggling to survive. The political instability that is holding the economy hostage is jeopardizing the print media, which is forced to jump on the Internet train.

For some, the Haitian press is in full evolution, for others it is in full crisis.

One or the other conclusion can hold the road depending on the glasses with which one looks at the area. However, we can add a third element: the Haitian media sector is full of paradoxes, not to say sprains, hindering its effective development. If the Haitian press has existed since the country's independence on January 1, 1804, as described in the first chapter of this book, we can, however, go back to the fall of the Duvalier on February 7, 1986, to understand the configuration of the media sector as it is today.

The new constitution guaranteeing freedom of the press adopted in the aftermath of the end of the ferocious dictatorship largely explains the proliferation of electronic media. However, elements such as quality training centers to train qualified workers for the media, institutions to supervise the work of the media, the adoption of a code of ethics and professional conduct to counter abuses in the sector and the establishment of a reliable economic model for the media have not worked hand in hand with the proliferation of the media. Today, these essential ingredients for media consolidation are missing. This is partly the cause of the fragility of the Haitian media sector. To this, it must be emphasized that Haiti has been living in a spiral of crises since the fall of the Duvalier. This creates an environment hostile to the effective development of the media.

This book by Wisnique Panier is a great contribution to understanding the sawtooth development of Haitian media. This work has the merit of providing a new theoretical grid for understanding and studying Haitian media. Evolving in a particular environment, the Haitian media sector has its own characteristics explaining the difficulties of studying it from the available media analysis grids.

In essence, Chapter 2 of this book describes a Haitian media system dominated by radio, by a strong politicization and therefore a strong political parallelism, by a weak presence of the State, by a small market that condemns the media and journalists to precariousness, by a domination of the radio space by a particularly political elite and by a low level of professionalism. This system he also describes evolving in a country characterized by a high migration of its population to foreign countries, by the active participation of members of its diaspora in radio debate programs and other national debate spaces.

Also, the environment in which this system operates is characterized by recurrent socio-political crises, illiteracy, insecurity, poverty, corruption, a low level of education, a strong politicization of institutions, the domination of a cultural and economic elite, the centralization of political and economic life in the metropolis, etc.

Indeed, the researcher has demonstrated that the Haitian media system has transformed over the past 60 years under the influence of three factors: linguistic, political, and technological. It shows that this upheaval is reflected in major changes in the relations between the actors of the system (media, public, advertisers, sources of information, state, and non-state regulatory bodies), certainly. However, the author has come to the curious conclusion that the main features of the Haitian media system remain essentially unchanged, without being reconfigured despite the changes observed.

While it is true that theories have a universal character, they are also called to evolve, contradict, supplement, or refute. This book is part of this dynamic. It is not only a contribution to analyze and understand the Haitian media, but also the media sectors in a socio-economic situation like that of Haiti.

To this end, Chapter 5 of the book presents an analysis of the different models of media systems existing in the literature, the three models developed by Halin and Mancini (2004). At the end of his examination, the author concludes that the Haitian media system does not belong to any of the existing models. It is therefore in this perspective that he proposes this new model baptized: the model of the precarious system of democratic transition or the Haitian Model. His study shows that the models proposed by Halin and Mancini in particular are ill-adapted to the Haitian case.

Chapter 4 provides the reader with an overview of system theory or systems applied to the media, drawing on the work of Canada's leading professors, Jean Charon, Collette Brin, and Jean de Bonville, who works on the "Nature and Transformation of Journalism."

All in all, the Haitian model is already attracting the curiosity of researchers and is generating enthusiasm in the scientific and media world. The author of "The ethics of the media in the face of the power of money: the case of Haiti and France" published in 2013 has already presented the content of this theoretical proposal in some major annual scientific meetings in the field of communication and media studies. This new theoretical model will serve as a grid to analyze other media systems that have characteristics like that of Haiti. It is up to you, dear readers, to discover the theoretical depth of this book you are reading.

Jean Phares JEROME,
Master in Population and Development,
Professor at the State University of Haiti (UEH)
Journalist and columnist at the Journal Le Nouvelliste

INTRODUCTION

This book focuses on the transformation of the Haitian radio system during the years 1957 to 2020 and proposes a new theoretical model of media system called: Haitian model, or the model of the precarious system of democratic transition. It stems from our doctoral thesis aimed at examining how the relationships between the different actors of the Haitian media system have changed over the past sixty years and identifying the explanatory factors of this change. More specifically, it is a question of determining to what extent the various changes made in the system lead or not to a reconfiguration of the system. This book is both theoretical and didactic in nature.

Indeed, the configuration of the Haitian media system refers to the state of existing relations between the actors from the year 1957, which constitutes the starting point of our study. We will see that since that date, the Haitian media system was characterized by the domination of an elite in the media space, a domination of the media of Port-au-Prince over the others, a strong politicization of the media. Also, the global environment in which the Haitian media system operates is characterized by, among other things, recurrent political crises, corruption, illiteracy, and poverty.[1]

Depending on the changes observed, has there or has there not been a reconfiguration of the system? That is, a radical revolution in its fundamental characteristics? This is the main question answered by our study, which gave rise to this book. What are the main elements of the system that have changed from 1957 to 2020 and which have not? We have assumed that the relationships between the actors of the Haitian media system have changed under the influence of three sets of factors: linguistic, democratic, and technological over the past six decades.[2]

---

1. Haiti is ranked 168th out of 100 in the Corruption Perception Index published by the international NGO transparency on January 23, 2020, while it occupied the 161st place the previous year. This shows that corruption is gaining more and more ground in the country.

2. These three factors will be developed more broadly through other publications. This book is purely theoretical in nature.

Does this transformation of relations between actors lead to a reconfiguration of the radio system? A reconfiguration will occur if the deep nature, the fundamental characteristics, and the environment in which the media system evolves have changed to the point that they become unrecognizable by the actors. That is, if everything has been changed and rebuilt on completely new foundations. In fact, Haitian media, and other actors such as the public (local and diaspora)[3], news sources, advertisers, state, and non-state regulators form a complex system of relationships. That is, each of the actors occupies a certain position and maintains certain relationships of interdependence with the others. By definition, a relationship system is a set of actors linked by relations of interdependence and whose actions are coordinated by regulatory mechanisms that allow the whole to maintain itself" (Charron, 1990, 1). In the Haitian radio system, each radio station is defined or determined by and through its relationships[4] with other key players in the system. We therefore wanted to understand and explain this system of relationships to account for its main changes. Indeed, any system of concrete relations implies a power play between the actors who compose it. The interactions between the actors of the system we analyze are governed by what Charron and Le Cam (2008) consider to be a communication contract, that is to say by the "set of norms, conventions and reciprocal expectations that regulate public communication practices" (p. 19). Changes in relationships between the actors of the Haitian media system are also analyzed from the perspective of the public communication contract. In the case of Haiti, we have identified a clear set of facts that suggests several changes in the functioning of the media system. Such transformations affect all aspects of the functioning of the media in Haiti and in their relationship with news sources, advertisers, the National Association of Haitian Media (ANMH), the public, regulatory bodies, and state powers, etc.[5]

---

3. In general, the notion of "public" refers to all readers, viewers, listeners, or "receivers" of media messages. In our case study, the public concept refers to the listeners of Haitian radios.

4. Donati (2004) considers a relationship as a "specific object of sociology". He starts from the observation that the "object" of sociology is neither the "subject", nor the social system, nor any of the similar couples (action and structure, lived worlds and social system, etc.), but the social relationship" (Donati, 2004). Other researchers such as Rioux and Dufour (2008) analyze a relationship as "a dynamic link." It is, according to them, a relationship between an individual and one or more other persons, between an individual and one or more groups, between a group and one or more other groups. According to them, a relationship is dynamic due to the fact that it is a process of social integration that determines the place of each of the constituent elements of the relational system.

5. There are other associations of press bosses and many associations of journalists in Haiti. Nevertheless, these are the rather marginal associations, which are not representative or influential enough to require their integration into the system we are studying. However, in relation to its influence and national representativeness, the National

For methodological reasons, we focused our study on traditional Haitian radio with its extension to the Web. We will see that radio is the dominant media in Haiti in the sense that it represents the main technical and institutional mechanism for public communication in the country. We will note that this domination of radio is due to many factors, such as illiteracy and the culture of oral education that characterizes Haiti.

The Haitian radio system is therefore a subsystem of the overall structure of Haitian media that we define as all media (radios, televisions, written press), legally registered or not with the Haitian State, or created by Haitian or foreign citizens and registered with a foreign state, operating legally or illegally, provided that these media particularly serve a Haitian community in Haiti or the diaspora.

To this end, the concept of "Haitian radio" also refers to all Haitian radio stations that serve the inhabitants of Haiti and/or Haitian communities in the diaspora. The latter refers to all Haitians living permanently outside Haiti, scattered throughout the world, who create community ties amongst themselves, who claim a Haitian identity, and who maintain a certain socio-cultural, political, and economic relationship with Haiti.

The purpose of this book can be defined as being, on the one hand, a presentation of the fundamental characteristics of the Haitian media system. And, on the other hand, a proposal for a new model that characterizes the Haitian media system. We call this new model: *the model of the precarious system of democratic transition* because we conclude that the Haitian media system does not correspond to any of the three theoretical models presented by Hallin and Mancini (2004). In summary, the subject of this book is gradually constructed in the light of the scientific literature on the issue and according to our direct and indirect observations, interviews, and our personal experiences as actors or as part of the groups of actors of the observed system.

Without wishing to exclude or minimize other actors, we deal much more in depth with the relationships between four main actors of the Haitian radio system, namely radio and journalists, news sources, the public and advertisers. My experience as a journalist and as a wise listener has served us well in this process. We systematically observe the debate programs, the news editions, as well as the "Guest" sections of the radios to identify the changes in the relations of the actors of the system which are particularly related to digital technologies.

Association of Haitian Media (ANMH) (A note in a note?) is considered a strong regulatory body even in the absence of the application of formal rules such as a code of ethics within the profession.

It is based on all of this that we have built our research object with the aim of advancing knowledge in the field of public communication in the light of the particularities of the Haitian radio system.

In this book, we will see that those digital technologies as well as linguistics, economic, and political factors are important elements in the transformation of relations between the actors of the Haitian radio system. Media systems around the world are constantly evolving under the influence of different factors. The use of digital tools by the actors of the Haitian radio system becomes an almost natural activity that impacts the system and accelerates the process of its transformation. Over the past fifteen years, there has been a set of new digital applications that facilitate or participate in the modification of relationships between actors.

In this study, we consider digital technologies to be a determining factor in the transformation of the Haitian radio system, particularly in the evolution of the relationships between the different actors that make up the system. "We say numerical information that is in the form of numbers associated with an indication of the physical quantity to which they apply, allowing calculations, statistics and verification of mathematical models. Digital is opposed in this sense to *analog* and *algebraic*" (Wikipedia 2020) This concept has been used to define new forms of sound recording, images, or videos.

Digital technologies cover a multiplicity of practices. Their scope of application goes beyond even its world. It also applies to telecommunications and the internet. Nevertheless, in our work, we consider the different technological tools used by the actors of the Haitian radio system in their daily practices. We consider phone calls and messages transmitted using digital applications or social networks such as: WhatsApp, Facebook, SMS, and other applications used by actors in their relational practices. We will see that this digitally accelerated transformation is part of a process of change that was already underway.

We take into consideration three main periods in the process of transforming the Haitian radio system. The first period spans the entire duration of the Duvalier dictatorship from 1957 to 1986. This is the period of total denial of freedom of expression and the press in the country. This is also the period during which Creole was gradually used as a language of communication in news editions and public debates in Haiti.[6]

---

6. This is an approximate date, as the sources are contradictory. The various sources show that information in Creole began to be disseminated between 1973 and 1976.

The second period extends from February 7, 1986, which corresponds to the date of the fall of the Duvalier dictatorship, to December 16, 1990, which postponed the organization of the first democratic election in the country that brought to power the Catholic priest Jean-Bertrand Aristide. It is the period of political instability that paves the way for democracy in the country. It was also from 1986 that there was a liberalization of public speech, the beginning of the multiplication of the number of radios, and the amplification of the use of Creole in radio, as we will see later. We begin the third period from 1992, which marks the arrival of the internet in Haiti, which we consider as a period of great acceleration of the transformation process or great changes in the relations between the actors of the radio system. The arrival of the mobile phone in the country in the 2000s and the beginning of the presence of some radios on the Internet also contributed to the transformation of the system.[7]

The different media systems are evolving considerably. In reviewing the main works on the evolution of media systems and changes in the relationships between actors, we found the existence of a large gap to be filled in the literature. The main works on media systems and their evolution (Hallin and Mancini, 2004; Brin, Charron, and de Bonville, 2004)[8] do not address the question of change in the relations between actors in the context of the development of digital technologies let alone on the basis of linguistic and democratic considerations. This is a pioneering work on the changes in relations between the actors of the Haitian radio system from the establishment of the first radio station in Haiti in 1928 to the digital age.

No study has yet focused on the transformation of the Haitian radio system. Also, the specific case of Haiti with radio as the dominant media, as well as its social political context of development can contribute to advancing knowledge in the field of public communication. One of the reasons for this is our study. Despite the evidence of changes in the relationships between the actors of media systems with the development of digital tools, the literature on this issue is still very poor. In the specific case of Haiti, media research is almost existent. Research on the impact of digital technologies, on political participation, and on the composition of public media spaces is numerous. However, little has been said about how these technical devices contribute to the transformation of

---

7. It should be noted that the first concession for the exploitation of the internet in the country was granted to the company Alpha communications Network (ACN) in 1995.

8. We will come back to this in the theoretical framework.

relations between actors in radio systems, particularly in less developed countries such as Haiti. The interest of our research lies above all in the fact that the transformation of the Haitian radio system remains unexplored while radio is increasingly asserting itself as the dominant media in Haiti, and that the participation of Haitians in the diaspora in public debates held from their country of origin is becoming more and more intense.[9]

Since the fall of the Duvalier dictatorship, freedom of expression has been the best guaranteed right in the country. Radio is the main place of public debate, the main technical device of public communication that promotes the full enjoyment of this right, whether for the actors of power, for the political opponents, or for all the citizens of the country. Radio is the backbone of democracy in the country. It is rooted in the daily life of the Haitian people in the sense that it is the media of proximity par excellence in the country. In addition to its contribution to the advancement of knowledge in media studies, this study will allow the various actors of the Haitian radio system to better understand the changes in their relationships, and to better understand the foundations of the social ties created by radios.

Fields of Application

We were interested in news radio as a tool for mass communication. More specifically, we were interested in the editions of short stories, and public debates and discourses that circulate within the Haitian public radio space, and the different types of relationships that actors maintain. Thus, our research work is part of the field of public communication in the wake of studies relating to the transformation of media systems, public participation in radio debate programs, and the use and influence of digital technologies on media systems.[10]

Indeed, there are several ways to define the concept of public communication. Nevertheless, we adopt the definition proposed by the Department of Communication and Information of the Faculty of Arts of Université Laval, namely: "public communication" includes: "all the phenomena of production, processing, dissemination and feedback of information that reflects, creates and

---

9. Digital technologies can be understood as the implementation of computer applications in the daily lives of individuals and the organizations that make use of them.

10. The notion of a media system will be developed a little further.

guide debates and public issues; public communication is not only the work of the media, but also of the institutions, companies, movements and groups that intervene in the public square" (Beauchamp, 1991, p. XII). According to Demers (2008), "public communication," as defined by the DIC, advances very closely to mediatized communication. According to him, there is a tradition in the Department that places the media, whatever they may be, at the center of researchers' concerns.

> Public communication refers first to all the messages transmitted by the communication media and to these media themselves. It also refers to the relationships that are established during the transmission of messages between individuals considered citizens. It affects not only public affairs and political life in general, but also all the problems facing society, and which are subject to public debate, agitate public opinion or fall within the remit of the state and public administration: economy, justice, education, health, environment, etc.
>
> (de Bonville, 1991, 4, cited by Demers, 2008, 211)

Given this definition, our research topic fits well with this concern. There is a very close link between public communication and the subject we are working on. Therefore, the transformation of the Haitian radio system that we analyze in this study is at the heart of the field of public communication as it is defined. In the European context, public communication is seen rather in the sense of State Public Relations, i.e., the communication actions implemented by public service institutions to communicate with target audiences.

Overview of Theoretical Perspectives

We have included this study in a multiple theoretical perspective. We use several different theoretical approaches in a logic of complementarity. First, it is the notion of a system that allows us to analyze the changes in the relations between the actors of the Haitian radio system. However, within this media system, there is a set of public debates, exchanges between the different actors. This public debate between the actors takes place in the context of the transformation or evolution of the radio system due to the use of digital tools by the actors. And somewhere, this transformation of the media system changes the conditions for participation in public debates. The question of public debate is part of our research problem.

So, to analyze these exchanges between the actors, we need the concept of public space. The peculiarity of the Haitian public space is that a large part of this public is outside the borders of Haiti. It is the diaspora that actively participates, directly and instantaneously, in the national political deliberation. The problem is that this part of the Haitian public has a dual belonging in the sense that it also intervenes in another public space, which is that of its host country. To analyze the relations of this component of the public with the Haitian media, we use transnationalism, which is an approach used in the field of international migration studies. It allows us to shed light on a specific aspect of our study, or another object, which is the participation of the Haitian diaspora in the Haitian public debate that systemic analysis and the concept of public space do not allow us to analyze. The system, transnationalism, and public space are indeed concepts that reflect different realities but are necessary to analyze the transformation of the Haitian radio system in the digital age. Changes in the relations between the actors are analyzed from the point of view of the public communication contract, i.e., the rules that weave the relations or exchanges between the actors of the radio space.

This book is divided into six chapters. The first chapter consists of presenting a portrait of the traditional Haitian media landscape (radio, television, and written press). This is a historical overview that allows us to better understand the socio-political and economic context in which the Haitian media operate. In the second chapter, we expose the main characteristics of the Haitian media system and its environment. The third chapter provides an overview of the factors explaining the transformation of the Haitian media system over the past sixty years. In the fourth chapter, we review the notion of the system and its main characteristics based mainly on the work of Charron and De Bonville. Through chapter ix, we present a summary of the main comparative studies of media systems, notably those of Hallin and Mancini (2004). And finally, we present in Chapter six our theoretical proposal, which is the model of the precarious system of democratic transition.

CHAPTER 1

Historical Overview of the Haitian Media Landscape

In this chapter, we paint a portrait of the Haitian media landscape from its inception to the present day. Because even if we have been interested in a period that begins in the 1950s, it is useful to understand what is happening in this period to place it in a broader historical context. We place particular emphasis on broadcasting, which interests us much more in this book. We also explain the dominant role of radio in the Haitian media system.

The Origins of the Haitian Media

The history of the Haitian media is as old as that of the Republic of Haiti. And we see that the written press existed well in the country long before the birth of Haiti. The former French colony gained its independence as the world's first Black Republic on January 1, 1804, following a general slave uprising against the slave system. Nevertheless, the press had existed in the colony of Santo Domingo for about eighty years before the birth of the Haitian nation. According to Desquiron (1996), the first media established itself in Haiti in 1724. It was the French journalist, Joseph de Payen, who founded the first newspaper in the colony under the name "Journal de Payen." Nevertheless, the arrival of this media in the French colony of Santo Domingo did not receive a favorable reception from the colonial authorities of the time. Its founder was imprisoned by the colony's governor, Rochelard, who destroyed his equipment and sent him back to France. It was not until forty years later that a second newspaper appeared in the colony. It was "La Gazette de Saint-Domingue," which was founded by the publisher Marie Antoine. Just like the first one, it wasn't going to last long. It was closed by Versailles since its title, the Santo Domingo Gazette, was deemed too devastating.

According to Desquiron (1996), there was a great resemblance between the Haitian press in its early days after Haiti's independence and the colonial press. The authoritarian temperament of the first Haitian heads of state (Emperor Jean-Jacques Dessalines, King Henri Christophe, Alexandre Pétion) did not favor the existence of a free press in the country. Desquiron stressed the fact that it was in Santo Domingo that the first press crime of the American continent was sanctioned, and it was also the Haitian State that was the author of the first murder of a journalist in the Americas. "Throughout its history the press has been persecuted: closure of newspapers, imprisonment/or exile of journalists. We have seen, in modern times, the boiling journalist Jolibois perish in a dungeon to which he bequeathed his name; Louis Callard died under torture; Georges Petit knew twenty times the prison since the American occupation until the reign of Duvalier" (Desquiron, 1996, 3). Desquiron cited several other examples of journalists who were killed, exiled, sentenced to death in the line of duty long before the arrival of François Duvalier. A very short article published by the online newspaper, AlterPresse (2008) shows that since Haiti's independence in 1804 through 1825, the columns of newspapers were constantly fed by military mobilizations. After 1825, the press emphasized the struggle for freedom of expression, the protection of domestic trade from foreign competition, and criticism of the administration of President Jean-Pierre Boyer and his senior officials. In this article, it is specified that from 1843 to 1850, media content was particularly marked by internal conflicts in the newsrooms.

All this is to say that from its beginning and throughout its evolution, the Haitian press has evolved in very difficult conditions. This calamitous situation did not improve with the American occupation of 1915. Because, according to Desquiron, it was during this period that there was the arrest of a greater number of journalists, but also the subsequent adoption of three laws to limit press freedom. Some scholars, such as sociologist Sauveur Pierre Étienne (2007), consider the American occupation from 1915 to 1934 as "a consequence of the collapse of the Haitian state" because it was not able to provide appropriate responses to the various socio-economic problems that gave rise to major socio-political conflicts in the country.

The Written Press: An Elitist Media in Decline in Haiti?

Before François Duvalier took power, the written press was undoubtedly an important media in Haiti without necessarily being dominant since the population was mostly illiterate. There were no less than seven daily newspapers and fifty-four periodicals in the country at the beginning of the dictatorship [Roc Pierre Louis, 2020]. Nevertheless, they gradually disappeared under the repression of dictatorial power. Today there are only two Haitian dailies of national circulation, the newspaper, *Le Nouvelliste*, founded in 1898, which is the oldest of the Haitian media, and the newspaper, *Le National*, founded in 2015. The written press in Haiti has always been an elitist medium that only addresses a small part of the population.

There are two major reasons for this. On the one hand, according to available statistical data, in 2017, the youth literacy rate was 70.5% [Unicef, 2017]. Even if the newspapers were written in Creole, the same problem would still arise, unlike the radio. On the other hand, the literate minority faces economic difficulties. A monthly subscription to the newspaper *Le Nouvelliste*, for example, costs about 200 gourdes, about 2 US dollars, which seems like a lot in a country where the unemployment rate is 45.5 percent in the metropolitan area and 28.2 percent in provincial cities. For those who work, the minimum wage per eight-hour working day is between 175 gourdes and 340 gourdes, depending on the category or type of job. This gives an average monthly salary of 7725 gourdes, or about 75 US dollars. Because of this economic precariousness, only a tiny part of the literate population can afford the luxury of having a subscription to a newspaper. It is true that the newspaper has an online version accessible to all free of charge, but because of the problem of illiteracy and the lack of access to the internet, it is still only a minority that can benefit from it. Valery Daudier said that the newspaper *Le Nouvelliste* has only 20,000 subscribers out of a population of eleven million inhabitants.[1]

---

1. Remarks taken from his speech as part of the launch conference of the Center for Interdisciplinary Studies on Haitian Media on September 15, 2018, at Laval University. He is the editorial secretary of the newspaper Le Nouvelliste.

A Brief Look at the History of Broadcasting

Radio as we know it today has a very long history. It is the culmination of a series of technological advances that have resulted in today's modern telecommunications system. Therefore, the discovery of radio is seen as a collective work resulting from different research works. Here we present a brief history of broadcasting in Haiti. This adventure began in Haiti in 1926, under the presidency of Louis Borno, with the first broadcasts of HHK radio, inaugurated on October 22, 1926. It transmitted on the AM band over a range of 830 KHZ, which is equivalent to 361.2 meters, with a power of 1 KW (1000 W). Subsequently, the 920 KC was preferred to the 830. The transmitter of this first radio station in the country was built by Western Electric. Its break-in broadcasts took place between July and August 1926. Note that according to Bastien and Hartt, "radio was introduced in Haiti for educational (propaganda) purposes by the American occupier. HHK, a station valued at $40,000, with a power of 1 kilowatt that broadcast for two hours (8–9) on Friday evenings special programs for peasants"[2] (Bastien and Hartt, 1980).[3] This program was also broadcast a few times from 6:45 a.m. to 7:15 a.m. on Saturdays, according to the details of Jacklin Jean-Paul. According to Sony Bastien, which reported a presentation by David Hartt, the main provincial cities were equipped with devices in front of public squares.[4]

By 1925, Americans had ordered about 150 receivers for rural schools across the country. Jacklin Jean Paul recalls that the HHK was much criticized because it was a station that broadcast American propaganda. This strategy is like the case of a country like Malawi, for example, where illiteracy and lack of access to sources of information excluded rural residents from the public media space (Mhagama 2015). They became "speechless," since they did not participate in any discussion forum and no media reported on them. In places where there were community radio stations, they created Radio Listening Clubs (RECs) to facilitate the participation of ordinary people in political life. Based on face-to-face interviews and group discussions, Mhagama (2015)

---

2. See *Le Nouvelliste*, Saturday, October 23, 1926 (quoted by Jacklin Jean-Paul). Note that for the most part, the information cited in this section was collected by Jacklin Jean-Paul for the purpose of his book entitled, "Haiti 100 Years of Broadcasting," which is forthcoming.

3. Pastor David Hartt, founder of Radio Lumière, is the first to carry out work on the history of broadcasting in Haiti.

4. This is a summary of the text by Pastor David Hartt, founder of Radio Lumière, on the History of Broadcasting in Haiti, presented as part of the fourth working session at the International Summer Course in 1980.

analyses how these listening clubs enabled rural residents to participate in public media debates.

Radio has not been a valid competitor for the written press despite the latter's elitist nature. Because, according to Jean Desquiron, the price of radio receivers was very high. They were not within the reach of most of the population. In addition, the programs were not attractive enough and the radio stations broadcast only in French. Over time, there was only one "advertisement in Creole of small size," and a few rare programs in Creole that Jean Desquiron describes as folkloric. According to Jacklin Jean-Paul , the Haitian government made a concession on June 9, 1938, to the Société Auxiliaire d'Études et de Gestion for the arrival of a new operator in the broadcasting sector in Haiti. Based on this agreement, a radio station and a television channel in the country was to be created. Based on this contract, the Haitian State had granted a group of French investors from the Thomson-Ho Company the monopoly of the sector.

The Birth of the Haitian Broadcasting Corporation

Jacklin Jean-Paul (2019) considers the creation of the "Haitian Broadcasting Company" as a "commercial necessity." He specifies that the Company Mallebranche, Gentil, Bogat and Co S.A (MAGEBCO) became the exclusive representative of the radio Electrola RCA-Victor in Haiti from 1932. This allowed them to "sell receivers, phonograph springs, phonograph records of artists, including Jimmie Rogers, and bands like Trio Matamoros, etc." He wondered why the receivers were sold in the absence of local stations operating daily. That was a real problem. According to Jean-Paul (2019), it was Armand Mallebranche, one of the founders of MAGEBCO, lawyer Henry M. Borno, merchant Robert Nadal, engineer Roger Armand, and architect Philippe Brun who would find the solution to this equation by founding a company with a capital of four thousand dollars, divided into eighty shares of fifty dollars each called *Société Haïtienne de Radiodiffusion*. The decree authorizing the operation of said company was disclosed in *Journal Le Moniteur* on December 2, 1935. Following the details of its statutes published in the *Journal Le Moniteur*, the station of the Haitian Broadcasting Company was founded on July 9, 1935. According to Jean-Paul, in 1948, HH2S, which was born on May 1, 1935, became Radio Port-au-Prince S.A. This radio station, according to Sérant (2007), is the "first private radio experiment" in the country.

HH3W Broadcasting Station: A Personal Satisfaction

Jacklin Jean-Paul considers the founder of the second private radio, HH3W, Ricardo Widmaier, as "a notorious handyman" who wanted to do radio for rather personal reasons. Its innovative ideal and above all its perseverance gave birth to HH3W, a radio set that, until the beginning of the decade 2000–2010, still broadcast. It would a few years later (1941–1945) compete with two other radio stations, HH3W, owned by Ricardo Widmaier, and HHBM which was renamed MBC. The HH3W was inaugurated on the 6135 kilocycles (or on the 48.90-meter strip) on Thursday, November 7, 1935. It broadcast on short waves. This program designed under "the patronage of Ludovic Lamothe" was dedicated to the Haitian Press (Jean-Paul, 2019).

Note that in the 1950s, HH3W became Radio Haiti. In September 1971, it was renamed Radio Haiti Inter. Other authors such as Vario Sérant indicate that there were a dozen new radio stations in Port-au-Prince between 1948 and 1955 including Radio Caraïbes, which is currently the most popular radio in the country and the oldest in Port-au-Prince. Also, a dozen other radio stations were created in other provincial cities before 1958. "The era of the transistor explosion in Haiti (1957–1967) coincided with the strengthening of the dynamism of the first denominational radio stations" (Sérant 2007, 41). According to him, it was in 1950 that the first denominational radio, 4VEH began its broadcasts. In 1959, its installed capacity was already ten kilowatts/hour on 1035 kHz. Also, Radio Lumière, which began broadcasting in 1958, had a power of one KWH on 760 kHz. Initially, radio was reserved for an elite who had the ability to obtain a receiver device.

> After the war, the transistor changed all this by making the radio accessible to the large number and in the most remote areas thanks to small dry batteries. The transistor allowed the advent of the speaker addressing the masses in a language they understand, Creole. The power immediately saw that these journalists who spoke to the people (nan lang manman li), bypassing the print, represented a new species that it considered more dangerous than the writer journalist with his limited audience.[5]
>
> (Desquiron 1997, 5)

---

5. This means his mother tongue.

Since the arrival of the transistor in the country, radio gradually established itself as the dominant media in Haiti. Despite the arrival of many televisions and written newspapers, as we will see later, radio remains the most accessible medium for most of the Haitian people. If we stay in the small history of broadcasting in Haiti, Jacklin Jean-Paul recalls that the HHBM, which was renamed radio MBC in 1944, was still the oldest radio station in operation in the country until January 12, 2010, before the powerful earthquake that killed more than 250,000 people. He recalls that this station was founded by the young Franck C. Magloire, director and son of Clément Magloire, owner of the daily newspaper, *Le Matin*. According to Jean-Paul, Mr. Magloire was excited about the success of the HH2S and the HH3W. He obtained the necessary authorization for the operation of his station on November 4, 1940. Test broadcasts for this station began on February 23, 1940, a month before its inauguration. It should be noted that between 1944 and 1949, stations such as HHYM, HHCP, and HHCN also emerged in the country. And in 1949, the 4 V area code came into force as a replacement for the HH.

A Look at the Evolution of Television in the Country and its Inaccessibility to the Public

Télé-Haïti (TH), which was established on December 13, 1959, was the first television station to set up in the country. Then came Haiti's national television (TNH), which was set up by the president for life Jean-Claude Duvalier in 1979. Until the fall of the dictatorship, television remained the exclusive prerogative of a privileged elite. The DAGMAR (2010) study shows that until 1989, there were still only two television channels in the country. But three years later, in 1992, that number quickly grew to thirty-two on-air television channels across the country. According to data collected by IHSI, "most television channels, which numbered 55 in 2008, are sole proprietorships (79%). Only 13% are corporations and 8% have not declared status. They are community and religious channels" (IHSI, 30). In 2015, the number of television stations increased further. It has risen to ninety-four across the country, including thirty-six in Port-au-Prince, said (Altéma 2016). In 2019, the National Telecommunications Council (CONATEL) clarified that the number of television stations in the country is 167, of which 111 are officially recognized. According to to the IHSI report [2008], the education and entertainment of viewers are the primary concerns of television stations. "Versed in amateurism, television remains rickety and anemic in Haiti" (Pierre Louis 2011, p. 22). Why so many TV stations in the country? In fact, most radio owners also held a license to operate a television channel.

The National Telecommunications Council (CONATEL), which is the sole regulatory authority for telecommunications activities in Haiti, including broadcasting, has given licensees a period to put their television on the air or risk losing this license. To keep this operating license, their owners rushed to put their television on the air even in the absence of the necessary basic infrastructure. For this reason, their programs have revolved around sports, cinema, and music videos of popular music artists. "70% of retransmissions are in French and 30% in Creole for commercial and public television, while a distribution of 80% in Creole and 20% in French is observed for the community and religious television" [IHSI, 2009, p. 31]. Even if the owners of the TV stations had ways to make them work properly, they would not get a large audience. As has been said, the country faces an almost chronic electricity problem. In addition, most people cannot afford to stay for long hours in front of the TV.

The Regulation of Broadcasting in Haiti

In Haiti, radio stations, like other media, maintain relations with state and non-state regulatory bodies. CONATEL is the main public regulatory body for broadcasting in Haiti. It was created by the decree law of October 30, 1969, set out by the former president for life, François Duvalier. Article 2 of the decree places CONATEL under the supervision of the Ministry of Public Works, Transport and Communication (Duvalier, 1969). According to Article 7 Paragraph A of this decree, "the main activities of the National Telecommunications Council are to: l) regulate and control Telecommunications with regard to broadcasting—television—the distribution of frequencies according to the table of allocations of the International Committee for Frequency Registration (I.F.R.B.)—technical authorization for radiocommunication stations and control of installations under the conditions laid down by law" (Duvalier, 1969.2). Broadcasting in Haiti is regulated by articles 49 to 73 of the Decree-Law of 30, 1977, granting the Haitian State the monopoly of telecommunications services. According to Article 49 of that decree law, national broadcasting is divided into three categories: (1) state broadcasting (2) private broadcasting, including those of advertising and commercial nature and those of a cultural or religious nature, and (3) television "visual broadcasting" by coaxial cable or radio beam.

In the current context of the development of broadcasting in Haiti, we can say that this decree is not in line with current broadcasting circumstances in Haiti. Community radios or even Web radios are not even considered in this decree. There is therefore no law that regulates the operation of community radios and Web radio in Haiti.

All persons seeking authorization to establish a broadcasting station in Haiti must follow the following procedure: first, they must apply for authorization from the Ministry of the Interior and Local Authorities (MICT). Then, they must send the station's technical file to CONATEL. And finally, applicants must pay the procedural costs and complete the related questionnaire. Once these formalities have been completed, CONATEL checks whether the preliminary steps have been taken before proceeding to the analysis of the application file. CONATEL grants authorization to the applicant provided that his or her file is compliant and benefits from a favorable opinion of the Ministry of the Interior. It should be noted that licenses granted for religious, community, and educational radio stations are not authorized to broadcast advertising messages.

Regarding the procedures for putting a station on the air, CONATEL must approve the applicants' equipment. Once installed, the applicant must write to CONATEL so that the latter can verify the conformity of the installations with the license granted to the applicant. If everything is in conformity, CONATEL grants the applicant a period of eighteen months from the date of issue of the letter of assignment for test broadcasts. The license regulator must pay an annual fee to continue using the frequency granted to him or her.

Indeed, CONATEL's mission is to define and conduct the Haitian government's telecommunications policies. It is also called upon to act as arbitrator and to decide in the event of disputes between consumers and operators. Its role is also to enforce the various contracts that bind the Haitian State with operators in the field of telecommunications, and manage the Radio Frequency Spectrum, and to assess requests for concession authorization.

From 1885 to 1986, the Haitian press and the telecommunications sector in general were the subject of numerous legal provisions. For about a century, nineteen laws and decree laws were issued on the press and the telecommunications sector in Haiti. In general, this legal framework demonstrated the will of Haitian leaders to take control of the press. The first decree law of August 27, 1885, published in No. 44 of the Official Government Gazette, Le Moniteur, was issued by President Lysius Félicité Salomon Jeune. Solomon's legislation was followed by many other legal provisions on Haitian media from the regime to the regime. That said, other regulations would follow, "some to supplement and others to limit, revise or repeal certain previous provisions, or to create institutions appropriate to an ever-wider dissemination of information in our environment" (Ministry of Information and Communication, 1986).

To some extent, we can consider the National Association of Haitian Media (ANMH), the Association of Independent Media (AMI), the Association of Haitian Journalists (AJH), SOS Journalists, and the National Union of Haitian Press Workers (SNTPH), which has not been in office for a decade, as non-state media regulatory bodies. So far, there is not yet a specific self-regulatory body in the country with the power of sanctions, despite the adoption of a code of ethics by the main associations of bosses and journalists of the country under the aegis of the UNESCO office in Haiti since 2011. There is therefore no peer jurisdiction that could receive complaints from the public and sanction possible abuses or failures related to compliance with ethical standards.

In a national radio system, there is a public space that can be regulated by the state. We can consider, for example, the modalities of licensing the operation of the media by the CONATEL, such as the regulation of radio content by the public authorities, particularly the law on defamation that is currently being debated in Haiti. However, in our case study, we have a radio space that is expanding outside the national territorial borders. It then becomes very difficult if not impossible for the state to set the rules of the game or to put beacons in this discursive space by regulation, because the power of a state is limited to its borders.

Nevertheless, as we see, technological tools facilitate the mobilization of Haitian actors in the diaspora through mechanisms that are partly beyond the control of the state, because the latter can regulate radio, telephone, and internet companies on its territory. It is true that in a democratic country, the state can regulate certain things, but it cannot control the public space to the extent that it cannot control who says what in a public debate. With digital technologies, this possibility of state regulation is becoming increasingly weakened. Given this situation, we can assume that there is a change in the rules of the game. The nature of the citizenship issue is subject to change.

Considering the Haitian social context, many Haitians in the diaspora change their nationality when they can do so to benefit from certain advantages reserved for citizens of host countries. However, Article 15 of the Haitian Constitution of 1987 does not yet recognize dual Haitian and foreign nationality. Otherwise, the proposed amendments contradict the 1983 law still in force. Therefore, this law must first comply with the constitutional requirements. Haitians who take another nationality are therefore no longer legally Haitian citizens. However, for the media, they are still legitimate actors in the national public space, which is addressed to a state in which they no longer live. They can act without being sanctioned by Haitian law.

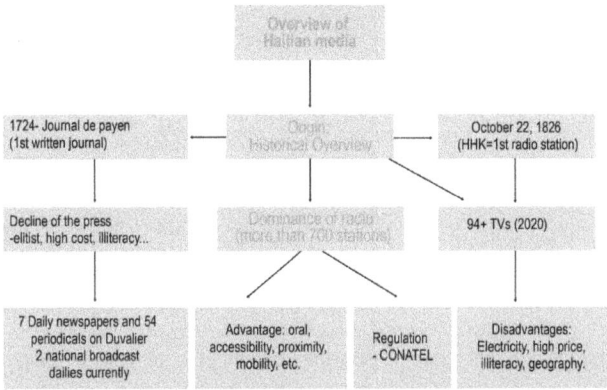

Figure 1. Panoramic presentation of Haitian media

Partial conclusion

In this chapter, we have given an overview of the Haitian media landscape. This allows us to deduce that the written press remains an elitist medium that is aimed at a crippled part of the Haitian population. On the one hand, it pays off and on the other hand, the illiteracy rate is still very high in the country. Despite the increase in the number of televisions in the country over the past two decades, television is still a very difficult media to access due to its high cost and the problem of access to electricity or the "blackout" phenomenon in the country. This means that radio remains the most accessible medium in the country.

CHAPTER 2

The Characteristics of the Haitian Media System and its Environment

In this chapter, we present the main characteristics of the Haitian media system and those of its environment. Any media system is dependent on the media and depends on the socio-political, cultural, and economic environment in which it operates.

The Fundamental Characteristics of the Haitian Media System

The Haitian media system has evolved in a very particular environment. A system depends on its environment. This implies that certain characteristics of the system are first and foremost those of the environment in which the Haitian media operates. These characteristics influence the functioning of the system and come to constitute rules of the game. Indeed, the Haitian media system evolves in an environment characterized by precariousness, a climate of recurrent insecurity, successive socio-political crises, illiteracy, and corruption.

The Fragility of Haiti's Democratic Institutions

Haiti's democratic institutions operate in a situation of almost permanent crisis. Serge Philippe Pierre considers Haiti as a "country in permanent crisis," a country turned toward contestation, confrontations, perplexity, anxiety, and economic malaise, etc. in a perpetual way. "After the departure of Duvalier, this country presented itself to the world as a nation in danger with itself, a nation in danger, unable to contain one's emotions and resentment in order to make the voice of reason, dialogue, forgiveness, conciliation and consultation heard" (Pierre, 2014, 14).[1] More than thirty years after the fall of the Duvalier regime, this situation remains unchanged. Very recently, Frantz Duval, news director of the newspaper, Le Nouvelliste, headlined his editorial dated July 20, 2016, "Will we be able to stop in time the general dysfunction of Haitian institutions?" (Duval 2016b). This is a wake-up call on the institutional problems currently existing in the country. Even institutions like CONATEL that set the rules of the game are themselves the subject of much debate.

This fragility of Haitian democratic institutions has great influences on the functioning of the Haitian media. "The Haitian press is what it is: the product of a given society, under the historical conditions that we know. It is puny, often formless, sometimes militant, sometimes analytical, with ups and downs" (Moïse 2013, 17). The Haitian media system is also characterized by an increasingly marked influence of Creole as a language of communication in radio since the 1970s which changes the media dynamic and the Haitian public space as we will see later in Chapter 5. In short, Haiti's entire history is marked by infighting for the seizure and maintenance of power and corruption in all its forms. The transition from dictatorship to democracy did not help the situation.[2]

Since the departure of Jean-Claude Duvalier on February 7, 1986, the country has been characterized by repeated political crises that have considerable impacts on the functioning of the Haitian radio system. We see that this political instability also leads to a proliferation of the number of radio stations in the country and political parallelism that contribute to transforming the system. Moreover, Haiti is a very poor country that lacks the resources to support itself. Its operating budget is financed by the international community, and a large part of its population relies on remittances from the diaspora to ensure its survival. As in all other countries, there is also the development of digital technologies that contributes to the transformation of the Haitian media system. Because of all of the above factors, we see which of the models presented by Hallin and Mancini (2004) actually fit the Haitian radio system.

---

1. It should be noted that in his doctoral thesis, Serge Philippe Pierre analyzes "the communication practices and strategies of government communication actors in Haiti, while taking into account the concerns of certain leaders from different sectors of society, as well as their posture toward this communication policy" (Pierre, 2014, 10).

2. See the chapters 3 (3.1) on the sociolinguistic factor and the one on the democratic factor of the transformation of the Haitian radio system.

The Economic Precariousness of the Actors of the System

Sources of revenue for the media are scarce and insufficient. The advertising market is cramped while the number of radio stations is multiplying. The meagre advertising market is controlled by a handful of radio stations grouped particularly within the National Association of Haitian Media (ANMH). There is many radios that work with very few resources. There is no public mechanism for funding media in the country other than government advertising. Radio craftsmen are, in general, underpaid. Journalists are paid a pittance.

A large part of the population is illiterate, and public debates are largely dominated by a literate elite. These conditions make the radio system vulnerable to corruption and political pressure, so radio is highly politicized. Due to its vulnerability, this system is subject to strong political pressures. It is therefore regulated by a politicization effect that is rooted in the very culture of Haitian society. The precariousness, insecurity, political instability, illiteracy, and corruption all also affect the other institutions of Haitian society: education, commerce, justice, and public administration, etc.

The past six decades have given rise to new conditions that have fostered certain changes in the Haitian radio system. Indeed, the valorization of Creole as a language of communication in radio, the process of democratization of the radio space since the fall of the Duvalier dictatorship, and the expansion of the radio system by digital technologies create new conditions and opportunities for the actors of the system. These environmental characteristics determine the operation of the radio system. These conditions become, from the point of view of the actors in the system, rules of the game.

This study reveals, however, that the structural conditions specific to the environment in which the Haitian media, particularly radio, operate create such inertia that, for the most part, the system, in its fundamental characteristics and in its nature, is maintained as such. The changes that can be observed in the relations between the actors do not lead to a real reconfiguration of the Haitian radio system. While there are some elements of change in the functioning of the system depending on linguistics, democratic, and technological factors, important factors of inertia explain why the system tends to maintain its fundamental characteristics.

Radio as the Dominant Media in Haiti

Radio remains the media that dominates the Haitian media system, the most accessible media. It is the main technical and institutional public communication system in the country. This is what justifies our choice to analyze the radio system as a subsystem of the Haitian media system. In November 2010, the market research company DAGMAR conducted a survey of 9907 people on media consumption in Haiti. This study found that 96% of Port-au-Prince residents listened to the radio daily. It shows that listeners spend their time listening time on news programs (64%), music (11.4%) religious programs (9.7%) sports programs (4.7%) (Dagmar, 2012).

A survey conducted by the IHSI in 2003, before the popularization of digital devices for radio reception, shows that there is a great disparity in media consumption in Haiti according to the type of media.

According to this survey, 47.6% of participants "reported listening to the radio in the week preceding the survey," less than 10% read the newspaper, and 18.2% watched television during the same period" (IHSI, p. 233). The proportion of people who listen to the radio is even higher in the metropolitan area of Port-au-Prince. "Listening to the radio is very widespread in the Metropolitan Area of Port-au-Prince (75.6%) and consequently in the West Department" (65.7%) (IHSI, 233). The DAGMAR survey showed that radio was the preferred source of information for 83.7% of respondents. Only 7.4% expressed a preference for television.

The popularity of radio as a media and mass communication is not a specifically Haitian reality. Here, we want to show that this reality that we observe in Haiti is also observed in other developing countries. A survey report conducted in 2015 by Farm Radio International among the population of five African countries shows that radio broadcast on AM/FM represents 86% of the hearing time of people aged between twenty-five and fifty-four years. Across the five countries in question, the percentage of radio hearings by gender has been distributed: in Mali, ninety percent of men and seventy-nine percent of women, in Ghana, eighty-seven percent of men and seventy-five percent of women, in Malawi, seventy-five percent of men and fifty-six percent of women, in Tanzania, eighty percent of men and sixty percent of women; in Uganda, eighty-six percent of men and seventy-two percent of women. They consume eight times more AM/FM radio than satellite radio and seventeen times more than internet audio streaming (Bartholomew 2011, 5). According to statistical data compiled by UNESCO, the number of radio stations around the world stands at 44,000 and seventy-five percent of households in developing countries have access to radio (UNESCO, 2019).[3] Based on the EFA Global Monitoring Report (2012, p. 290), UNESCO states that together with radio, mobile phones are the easiest technology to access, equipping more than 70% of the world's population).

This shows that, just like in Haiti, traditional radios are still very popular in developing countries. In Haiti, almost all issues of general interest are mainly discussed on the radio. It is commonplace par excellence for exchanges, discussions, or contradictory debates on subjects of public interest. It is the most powerful means of mass communication in the country. The characteristics of radio in Haiti make it the best tool of popular demand and a high place of exercise of freedom of expression guaranteed by the Constitution and the laws of the country. The debates that passthrough newspapers or television affect only a small minority of the population for several reasons that we will explain later.

Explanatory Factors for the Dominance of Radio

What explains the dominance of radio in the Haitian media system? The preponderance of radio is linked to certain characteristics of the socio-economic and cultural environment in which it operates. We explain this dominance according to four factors.

Cost and Free Radio

The first factor is due to the cost of the receiver and the free radio. Unlike television and print media, which is more difficult for an average Haitian to access, radio is within everyone's reach. With very little money, every household or even every individual who wants to can buy a small radio receiver at a low price. It just takes two small batteries to run a device that doesn't cost much. In addition, a large part of the mobile phones sold on the Haitian market are equipped with an AM/FM radio receiver. This means today in the development technological context, we listen to radio on his phone, so everyone can get a small radio receiver. In this case, radio is much more accessible.

---

3. See http://www.unesco.org/new/fr/unesco/events/prizes-and-celebrations/celebrations/international-days/world-radio-day-2013/statistics-on-radio/

No Access to Electric Currents

The second explanatory factor concerns access to the electric current. We are in an underdeveloped country where access to electricity is increasingly becoming a luxury. Unlike television, radio receivers work with dry batteries that are not too expensive. There are a multitude of radio stations in the country that can be received for free. Even if the TV programs are also free, there must be electricity, because the television does not run on a battery. In the absence of the electric current produced by the Electricity of Haiti (EDH), solar panels, batteries, or generators are needed to supply a television with electricity. All of this can be very expensive. Out of 137 countries, Haiti is ranked as the third-worst country in the world when it comes to access to electricity, according to the latest report published by The Spectator Index in 2017. It came behind Nigeria, which is in the second position and Yemen, which is a country in a state of war. This poor position in the ranking can be explained by the recurrent power cuts in the country or by the absence of electricity in several places. Haiti is the only territory in the Western Hemisphere where only thirty percent of the population (national average) has access to electricity and six percent in rural areas.[4]

Socio-economic Situation of the Country and Illiteracy

Thirdly, the unconditional attachment of Haitians to radio is also explained by the socio-economic situation of the country. Indeed, the high degree of illiteracy in the country can be seen as an explanatory factor for the dominance of radio in the country. "Haiti is a drifting country with nearly 80% illiterate. But since they are not stupid and still want to know, radio is the medium of choice" (Bonaparte, 1995, 114). The proportion of illiterates has declined significantly since 1995. Today, illiterate people make up less than forty percent of the Haitian population

---

4. Source: Haiti — "FLASH: Haiti 3rd worst country in the world in terms of access to electricity — HaitiLibre. com: All the news from Haiti 7/7/ 2017)."

Data		
Years	Values (%)	Variations (%)
1982	34.73	
2003	58.74	69.13
2006	48.69	-17.11
2016	61.69	26.70

Figure 2. Literacy level—adults (% of adults over 15 years of age
(World Outlook, 2020)

As shown in the table, the available statistical data shows that in 1982, the literacy level of Haitian adults over the age of fifteen was 34.73 percent. It increased to 58.74 percent in 2003. From 2003 to 2006, the literacy level fell to 48.69 percent before rising to 61.68 percent in 2016.). For the written newspaper, it's simple: most people can't read. Newspapers publish in French while most of the population is illiterate. This would not change much even if the newspapers were published in Creole.

Development of the Culture of Orality

The fourth factor is related to the development of the culture of orality in the country. Because of this problem of illiteracy, the population is developing a culture of orality. Many people do not read Creole or French, so the newspaper is intended for a small part of the population. This leads to the development of a culture of orality very advanced in the country. People listen to people talk more than they read. With all the difficulties of the country, French is not accessible to all, the cost of buying books or newspapers is exorbitant during radio costs almost nothing. This explains the success of radio in Haiti, in contrast to other countries where the dominant media is television and print media.

The Domination of Radio Space by an Elite

The strength of radio in Haiti is in principle to promote the dissemination of information, public debate, and the voice of all, regardless of whether people are literate or not, of course, but the democratic transition and the rise of Creole has not transformed the structure or fundamental characteristics of the radio system. There is indeed a certain democratization of the public radio space, the liberation of public speech, but this democracy has remained very relative. The radio space is still dominated by an elite, a political elite that exercises a certain hegemony, and an economic elite that controls the radio industry because of its ability to finance. Radio stations are mostly owned by political and economic actors. And since public debates essentially revolve around political issues, public speech is usually monopolized by political actors. Participation in certain forms of radio debate is, for all intents and purposes, reserved for this elite group who are often invited as experts in the "guest of the day" sections and in radio debate programs, or as protagonists of current events. Traditional forms of participation leave little room for ordinary people. It is in a few rare circumstances that the public or a specific category of the public is called upon to participate, except for certain open-mic programs. This means that the place occupied by this elite has not disappeared with the rise of Creole or with the change of political regime. As we explained in the previous chapter, the telephone has always been an important tool for participating in some public debate shows. However, from the fall of the dictatorship in 1986 until the 2000s, the telephone was still very elitist. Only a privileged minority had a landline or mobile phone at the end of the 1990s. This once again fostered the participation of an elite group on radio talk shows.

Even in large demonstrations or political mobilization movements in the streets, usually to demand the departure of any head of state, journalists always tend to identify the best-known personalities who are part of the particularly political elite, civil society, or the leaders of the movement to give voice to the cries of the crowd in the background. As Clarens Renois points out, "the political debate in the press has not advanced democracy. In Haiti, it is the one who shouts the loudest who is always right. It is the one who can frighten, who threatens and can kill who always has the last word" (Renois, 2016, 52). This observation by Renois makes sense in the Haitian context. Guests or participants in talk radio talk shows who are usually elements of the elite seek to intimidate, insult, and even come to blows. Even if the multiplication of the number of radio stations in the country opens the way to a multiplicity of points of view in the radio space and to the diversification of the choice of content for the public, there is still an educated minority that manages to impose itself in the public space to the detriment of members of the rather illiterate population. The changes recorded in the relations between the actors of the system are part of a social structure without revolutionizing it. There are therefore both elements of rupture and continuity.

The Politicization of the Radio System: An Element of Continuity

This study shows a strengthening of the politicization of the Haitian radio system despite the changes brought about by digital technology. This is a major challenge in the transformation of the system. From 1957 to 1986, the radio stations were under the yoke of the Duvalier dictatorship by very strict control mechanisms. This politicization of radio has not changed with the rise of Creole or with the fall of the dictatorship, let alone with the development of digital tools.

Radio remains a very powerful tool in the hands of political forces. Politicization, however, continues in another form. The changes observed are also part of a continuity of the basic structures of the system. For example, the politicization of the system is manifested first by the mode of ownership of radios. More and more of the country's political leaders are seeking to procure and own their own radio stations.

Then there is politicization by the mechanism of allocation of licenses for the operation of radios by CONATEL. Participants in our study were unanimous in asserting that radio licenses are granted largely based on political complacency whenever there is a change of government.

And finally, the Haitian radio system is politicized by its mode of financing. Corruption, covert financing, and ethical conflicts are also principles of regulation of the system. They characterize its mode of operation and maintain and solidify relationships of dependence and power. Some journalists receive public money with or without any specific communication mandate, while acting as arbiters in the public space, which is a form of politicization of radio. There are also many other forms of politicization that are described in this study, such as that by association.

This study shows, however, that there is a tension between, on the one hand, a highly politicized radio system, annexed to the political fields, and, on the other hand, a group of media bosses and journalists who demand autonomy of journalism and public debate from political forces. In short, the strong politicization of the radio system arouses certain resistance within the system itself.

In summary, this study leads to the conclusion that the Haitian radio system is not reconfigured despite the changes observed in the relations between the actors over the last sixty years. To conclude that the Haitian radio system had to be reconfigured, its fundamental characteristics and environment would have had to have been fundamentally changed. It would have been necessary that there had been a redistribution of power between the actors and that the radio, which was once an instrument in the hands of the Duvalier regime, became an autonomous institution capable of reporting on current events without political pressure, and of holding a more critical discourse in relation to political power, to the private business sector, and in relation to other political structures. There should have been a strong trend toward the professionalization of journalists, who would have sought to comply with ethical standards. Finally, with the valorization of Creole, democratization, and digital technology, we should have seen ordinary people access more freely to the radio space and thus defeat the domination of the public radio space by an elite.

A Strong Participation of the Diaspora in the Media Space

The Haitian media system is also characterized by a strong presence of Haitians from the diaspora in Haitian media spaces. One of the peculiarities of the particularly Haitian public radio space is that a large part of the participants in the national debates are outside the borders of Haiti. These are Haitians in the diaspora who are an important component of the Haitian public. This aspect is the subject of further analysis in the context of another publication that attempts to assess the influence of the diaspora in public debates. This work will be published both as a scientific article and as a work for the public.

This quantitative analysis of the interventions of members of the diaspora will allow us to arrive at a clearer estimate of the importance and influence of its participation. But this is part of the questions that we do not want to deal with widely in this book, which gives an outline to understand the Haitian media system. Also, this analysis will also allow us to determine to what extent the forces present in the diaspora are symmetrical compared to those based locally in Haiti, especially in relation to the elites who clear the radio space and the rest of the population or at least in relation to political groups and others.

We have observed an active participation of the diaspora in public debate radio broadcasts. One of the ways to observe it is in the context of certain types of programs, such as those with open mics or in discriminated forms of participation that, in some cases, give the floor only to people in the diaspora, depending on the subject under discussion. There are telephone lines that are reserved specifically for the diaspora. This participation is likely to be even greater in the context of the new forms of participation favored by digital technology. Our observations lead us to believe that there are many people in the diaspora who are exploiting the potential of digital technologies in their participation in public debates. In comparison with the public based locally in Haiti, there are many factors that play in favor of this diasporic audience such as: better access to electronic tools, better access to a broadband internet connection and electricity, and digital literacy, etc.

There are no figures on diaspora participation in radio talk shows. In this study, we did not conduct a quantitative analysis of its participation or a thematic analysis of public debates in depth. However, the assiduous listening to the program allows us to maintain that this participation is important and constant and that, in certain programs or on certain subjects, members of the diaspora are privileged speakers.

Along the way, we realized that to deal with this dimension at its true value, it would be necessary to open a vast survey of the diaspora and expand the scope of research in a way that seemed disproportionate to us. Diaspora participation is a complex issue that raises important issues, such as transnational identity, political participation in two national public spaces, the political influence of the diaspora, the pluralism of the diaspora itself, political cleavages within the diaspora itself (political parallelism, polarization), the political importance of the diaspora, and so on. So, we made the choice not to venture too far down this path, not because it was not interesting, on the contrary, but because it took us away from the central theme of our thesis, that of the configuration and reconfiguration of the radio system.

To better understand the problem of radio and the dynamics of public communication in Haiti, it would also be necessary to continue to explore other avenues of research such as the influence of radio on the political opinions of Haitians, the communication strategy of political parties, and the coverage of political issues by the main radio stations.

The typology of the forms of broadcasting and participation in radio debate programs that will be the subject of another publication has served us as an analytical tool and which we do not want to deal with in this book. The new forms of participation facilitated by digital tools are changing something in the dynamics of public debates since they facilitate greater participation. These are particularly the written forms of participation that are facilitated by digital tools. The transformation of the radio newspaper in Haiti is also an important avenue of research to explore. We have identified two extraordinary radio newspapers that we call "enfolodyans." A case study of these two editions of radio news would be very enlightening in view of the dynamics of radio transformation in Haiti.

This study also allowed us to see that WhatsApp Groups are an important tool for transforming the interdependent relationships between the actors of the Haitian radio system. Our observations have enabled us to establish that the analysts have set up a system of collaboration. And they themselves explained to us that technology allows them this collaboration that did not exist or less before. The new forms of collaboration facilitated by this digital tool would benefit from being examined much more in depth to better understand the constituent elements of this collaboration, its different forms of manifestation, and its impact on news coverage. It is from this perspective that we have chosen to deal with this aspect in another book.

The Characteristics of the Environment in which the Haitian Media System Evolves

Haiti has been characterized since its foundation on January 1, 1804, by a climate of recurrent insecurity, by successive socio-political crises, by corruption, and illiteracy, among other factor It is the poorest country in the Americas. It is in this environment that the Haitian radio system evolves. The main actors of the system are in a very precarious situation. Sources of revenue for radio stations are scarce and insufficient. The advertising market is cramped while the number of radio stations has multiplied since the fall of the Duvalier dictatorship. There is no public funding mechanism for private media in the country other than government advertising. Radio craftsmen are generally underpaid. A large part of the population is illiterate and public debates are largely dominated by a literate elite. These conditions make the radio system vulnerable to corruption and political pressure, so radio is highly politicized. Because of its vulnerability, this system is dominated by strong political pressures.[5]

---

5. In 2016, the adult literacy rate (+15) in Haiti is estimated at 61.7 percent. Source: https://knoema.fr/atlas/Ha%C3%AFti/topics/%C3%89ducation/Alphab%C3%A9tisation/Taux-dalphab%C3%A9tisation-des-adultes

Haiti's history, culture, and Creole language make it a lonely country in the Caribbean region or in the Americas. In his highly controversial book, "The Clash of Civilizations," Samuel P. Huntington considers Haiti "an isolated country" in the same way as Japan, which has nothing in common with other nations, or even their neighbors. "Haiti's elites were traditionally linked to France, but the Creole language, the voodoo religion, as well as its origins in the slave revolt and its turbulent history make this island an isolated country" (Huntington, 1997,195). We have good reason to believe that Haiti has political, economic, and sociocultural specificities that make its media system different. From this point of view, we can consider the Haitian media system to be unique. This makes it a fertile ground for research on the transformation of media systems.

The Haitian print media has evolved and is still evolving in a context of the decadence of the Haitian state and civil society structures. As Jean Desquiron noted, "it uses French, a language foreign to most of the population. Moreover, the shady power sees it with a very bad eye" (Desquiron, 1996, 2). Whoever wanted to have a newspaper in Haiti, he said, still had to prepare to face a multitude of difficulties such as finding unpublishable news and writing an editorial that was not likely to offend the government, the difficulties of having paid readers, having qualified collaborators, finding advertisers, and monitoring the composition, correction, and publication of the journal. A work that would require, according to Desquiron, exceptional qualities. Despite all these problems, no less than a thousand newspapers have been published in Haiti since its independence on the first of January 1804. Nevertheless, it is only the newspaper *Le Nouvelliste*, the current dean of the Haitian press, which has been able to resist until today.

Jean Desquiron has clearly demonstrated that, since its birth, the Haitian press has always evolved in a very difficult socio-economic and political context, a situation that has great influences in the process of the evolution of the Haitian media, particularly the radios that interest us in this study. The entire history of Haiti is marked by a fratricidal struggle for power, by successive coups d'état since the assassination on October 17, 1806, of Jean-Jacques Dessalines, the first head of state and founding father of the Haitian nation. Haiti experienced disastrous political turmoil in the decades leading up to François Duvalier's seizure of power in September 1957. Six Haitian presidents were assassinated in the interval of only four years, from 1911 to 1915. This led to a military intervention by the United States, which occupied the country in 1915, after the death of Haitian President Jean Vilbrun Guillaume Sam, until 1934. The Haitian political situation did not improve after the departure of the American occupiers in 1934. From 1946 to 1956 three presidents, Élie Lescot, Dumarsais Estimé, and Paul Eugène Magloire were ousted from power by coups. Military coups and riots continued to multiply in the country. François Duvalier came to power on September 22, 1957, following the popular uprising that led to the resignation of power of President Paul Eugène Magloire on December 6, 1956. To maintain his power, Duvalier established a regime of terror in the country by setting up a militia of the "Volunteers of National Security" (VSN) made up of 40,000 "tontons macoutes". He himself was the victim of nine coup attempts by his political opponents. Intellectuals, independent journalists, the Catholic Church in Haiti were in the crosshairs of François Duvalier.

François Duvalier's rise to power in 1957 took place following rigged elections. With the support of the Army and his personal militia (the Tontons Macoutes), he proclaimed himself president for life of the Republic of Haiti. This ferocious dictatorship cost the lives of thousands of opponents and the exile of thousands more. François Duvalier, known as "Papa Doc," died in 1971. His son Jean-Claude Duvalier, known as "Baby Doc," became president for life at the age of nineteen. Throughout the Duvalier dictatorship, the independent press was totally gagged. At the end of 1985, Jean-Claude Duvalier faced an unprecedented popular uprising. Many committed journalists braved the danger to support the anti-dictatorship protests that were often bloodily repressed. He went into exile in France on February 7, 1986, with his family.[6] "After the departure of the Duvaliers, Haiti presented itself to the whole world as a nation at war with itself. A few years after the fall of this regime, this country was constantly living in turmoil and the social atmosphere—politico-economic seemed heavy and unstable. Fear, insecurity, and mistrust have settled everywhere" (Pierre, 2014, 10). Until today, Haiti remains a young democracy that is still seeking its way after the long period of dictatorship of the Duvaliers, Papa Doc (1957–1971), and Baby Doc (1971–1986). In 1990, Jean-Bertrand Aristide became the first democratically elected president. Its institutional trajectory has been marked by major destabilizing movements. "Beyond Haiti's borders, we hardly hear about this new political crisis. Either the world is so used to seeing the country plunge into political chaos that it sees nothing new in it, or it has unfortunately lost all hope for it" (Chiara

---

6. See p.160, section: 6.5.2- Panier, Wisnique. 2021. «Les transformations du système radiophonique haïtien de 1957 à 2020: Changement et continuité». Québec (Québec): Université Laval, on the state of freedom of expression under the dictatorship.

2016). President Jean Bertrand Aristide was overthrown in turn on September 30, 1991, in a military coup. He went into exile in the United States before being reinstated to his post by the administration of President Bill Clinton, the former president of the United States. In 1996, he held elections that brought his former prime minister, René Préval, to power before being re-elected in 2001 for a second term. He was overthrown a second time on February 29, 2004, following protests to give power to a transitional government that lasted two years. In 2006, following a change in the method of counting blank votes, René Préval, a close associate of Jean-Bertrand Aristide, won the presidential elections with 51.15 percent of the vote. Victory was granted to him in a context of high tension and accusation of political opponents who denounced the irregularities that characterized the organization of these elections. Coming in second place, the Christian Democrat candidate, Professor Leslie Manigat, notably criticized the pressure of the international community and denounced a "coup d'état by the ballot box" in favor of his competitor.

Five years later, the Haitian singer, Joseph Michel Martelly, would win the second round of the presidential elections with 67.6 percent of the vote against 31.7 percent for Mirlande Manigat, the wife of Lesly François Manigat who is a former president of the Republic of Haiti. These elections were held in the wake of a terrible earthquake that killed more than 300,000 people in the country. Having been unable to organize the elections on time, Joseph Michel Martelly gave way to a transitional government chaired by the then President of the Senate of the Republic, Jecelerme Priver. His main mission was to continue the electoral process initiated under the presidency of his predecessor. The elections of November 20, 2016, brought entrepreneur Jovenel Moise to power with 55.6 percent of the vote, a year after postponing the second round of presidential elections that was due to take place in December 2015.

As in previous elections, the results of these elections were contested by the main candidates who denounced the irregularities. Implicated in a corruption scandal, President Moise faced popular protest movements demanding his departure from power. It is the context of the confinement linked to the development of COVID-19 that stopped the major protest movements against the current President of the Republic. All activities in the country were almost paralyzed during the two months preceding COVID-19 due to a movement called "Pays Lock" aimed at the resignation of President Jovenel Moise.

This study shows that Haitian society is characterized by recurrent political crises, a low level of education, poverty, corruption, insecurity, a strong politicization of institutions, the domination of a cultural and economic elite, and the centralization of political and economic life in the metropolis, etc. All these factors contribute to a certain inertia of the radio system. Is this conclusion on radio also valid for other institutions in Haiti that operate in the same context, including political institutions? For example, can the blockages in democratic construction in Haiti also be explained by the same factors of inertia?

For this purpose, the Haitian media system can be considered as an element of a large whole which is Haitian society considered as a global system. It is therefore possible that applying this scientific conception to each of the subsystems that structure Haitian society such as the education system, the judicial system, the political system, the economic system, and others, we will arrive at the same results. All Haitian institutions operate in the same global environment on which they depend.

We believe that the issue is even more complex. Some characteristics observed in the functioning of Haitian institutions based locally in Haiti are also observed through Haitian institutions of the diaspora, such as the media, commercial institutions, and public institutions such as diplomatic missions which, however, evolve in another environment with rules of the game that may be different. To this end, we hypothesize that the fundamental characteristics that structure Haitian society as a global system are maintained beyond national borders.

By observing the functioning of American, French, Canadian, or other institutions that evolve in Haiti, their mode of operation is not too different from those that evolve at the national level, in their country of origin. This leads us to another hypothesis that cultural factors exert a greater influence on the functioning of institutions than the physical environment in which they operate. In other words, the physical environment has little impact on the functioning of institutions. Rather, they are influenced by the legal, political, and socio-cultural environment of their country of origin, regardless of the physical environment in which they are located. For example, a Canadian institution in Haiti is not going to operate in the same way as Haiti and vice versa.

CHAPTER 3

The Factors Explaining the Transformation of the Haitian Media System[1]

In this chapter, we summarize the main factors explaining the transformation of the Haitian media system over the past sixty years. The factors in question are developed more broadly in our doctoral thesis and will be the subject of other publications. This book is rather theoretical in nature. We demonstrated in our doctoral thesis that the Haitian media system has transformed over the past sixty years under the influence of three sets of factors: linguistics, democratic, and technological. Nevertheless, this transformation is essentially reflected in the relations between the layers of the system. The fundamental elements that characterize the system and the environment in which it operates remain unchanged. They are part of the continuity of the system.

Linguistic Factor: Impact of Creole on the Radio System

The first explanatory factor for the transformation of the system is linguistic. The introduction of Creole to radio as a language of public communication from the 1970s onwards made it possible to put an end to the domination of French as the exclusive language of communication on radio. This had the immediate effect of ending the exclusion of most of the population from the radio space. The introduction of Creole to radio raised hopes for a change in the dynamics of public debate in the country and greater mobilization of the population against the Duvalier dictatorship. However, this hope of opening public space has come up against two major limitations. On the one hand, the rise of Creole did not prevent the Duvalier regime from flouting freedom of expression and controlling the dissemination of information and ideas through repression.

---

1. Here we give a brief overview of the explanatory factors of the Haitian media system over the last 60 years which are the main results of our doctoral thesis. These factors will be the subject of further publications in the form of scientific articles and books.

And on the other hand, there were technical limitations that excluded most of the population of public debate.

Subsequently, Creole can be considered as one of the conditions that have been gradually put in place to achieve several changes in the system, particularly in the practices of relations between actors. However, this condition does not play on its own; it brings other elements. The affirmation of Creole was fostered by a loosening of control of freedom of expression by the regime of Jean-Claude Duvalier, who was much more permissive than his father, and at the same time, the rise of Creole favored the fall of the regime through the mobilization of the popular masses. It was both an effect and a cause of the weakening of the dictatorship until its fall. Duvalier wanted to maintain his control, but the presence of Creole created a breach, which gradually favored a certain liberation of speech.

Democratic Factor:
Transition from Dictatorship to Democracy

The transition from dictatorship to democracy is a second fundamental factor in the transformation of the system. If Creole favored the fall of the regime, the liberation of speech began, to a certain extent, before the fall of the regime. But of course, the transition to democracy created a context of freedom in which protest speech was no longer repressed. The fall of the dictatorship on February 7, 1986, led to an increase in the number of radio stations and the creation of a multitude of popular organizations and political parties that changed the dynamics of public debate. This dynamic has not changed; it is still the elites who dominate the debates, and these debates carry only politics.

The combination of the fall of the dictatorship and the valorization of Creole favored the creation of certain democratic spaces in the system compared to the previous situation. The language of the dominated has taken over French in the public space. Radio content becomes directly accessible to the Creolophone masses. Radio debates and news editions are presented mainly in Creole. On the other hand, people who do not speak French can now intervene in radio debates in the language of the majority.

The rise of Creole and the democratic transition are very apparent realities. Yet they have not changed the structure or characteristics of the system as fundamentally as one might have thought. The changes are considerable, of course, but they do not lead to an upheaval of the basic structures of the system. The rules of the game have remained almost the same. Indeed, the dominated have remained dominated, even if the radio speaks their language.

The public radio space is still dominated by an elite that exercises a certain hegemony. This elite is particularly made up of intellectuals, political leaders, and professionals from different disciplines. Members of the economic elite have little presence in radio debates, but they act in the shadows. For radio, as an institution, is itself largely under the control of the economic and political elite, and it continues to operate according to a logic that serves the interests of this elite.

Political actors are omnipresent in the radio space because the public debate in Haiti fundamentally revolves around political issues, the taking and maintenance of political power. The other topics are relegated to the background. Creolization has not changed this situation. As a result, radio practices do not change, and it is practically the same actors who intervene in the debates.

Technological Factor: Impact of Digital Tools on the System

The use of digital tools by actors also contributes to the transformation of relations between the actors of the system. Some changes in the system are direct effects of the use of digital tools, particularly about the place and traditional role of actors in the system. The use of digital technologies may have removed some technical limitations related to public participation in debates. However, the fundamental characteristics of the system are not changed. Its nature is maintained as such.

Indeed, the various technical devices put in place since the 2000s have not changed the fact that public figures or elites remain the dominant actors in radio broadcasts. Certainly, digital tools promote the participation of ordinary people, but there is still an elite group that dominates the radio space. There are few technical limits to the participation of users of digital tools, but there are social, political, and cultural limits that still mean that it is a literate elite that dominates. Haitians in the diaspora become legitimate actors who intervene directly and instantly in Haitian radio debates. These diaspora participants, because of their socio-economic profile, can be considered a natural extension of this Haitian elite that dominates the radio space.

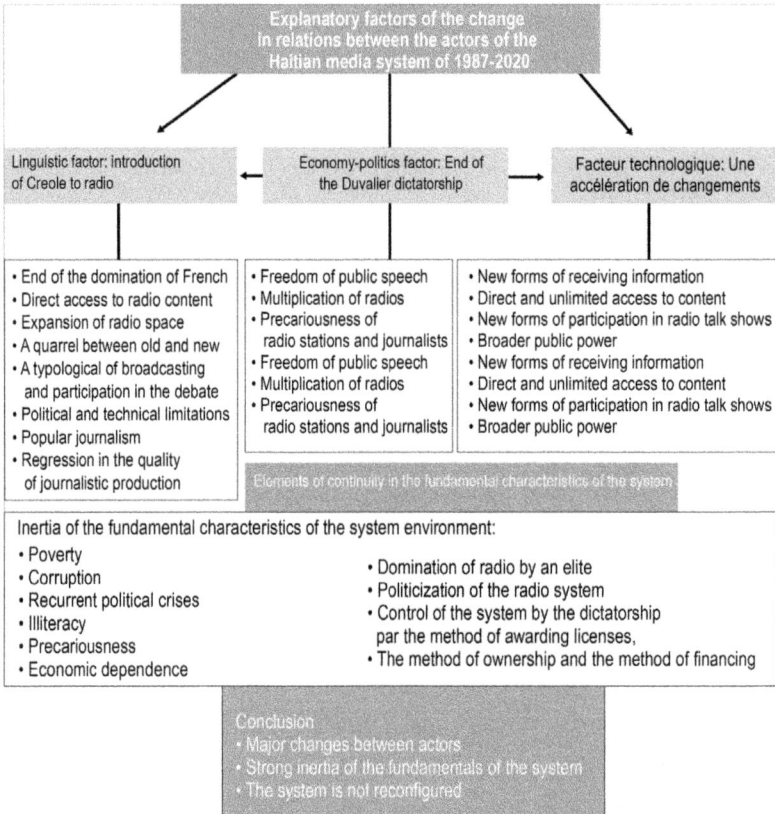

Figure 4. Summary table of the explicative factors of the Haitian media system.

CHAPTER 4

The Concept of System and Its Properties

In this chapter, we discuss the notion of a system applied to the media. This notion is fundamental to better understand the Haitian media system. We review the major properties and a system and the dimensions of the media system.

The System: A Definitional Approach

Ludwig Von Bertalanffy defines a system as "a set of interdependent elements, that is, linked together by relations such that if one is modified, the others are also modified and that, consequently, the whole is transformed" (Charron and de Bonville, 2002, 17). Systemic analysis, according to Charon and de Bonville, "focuses specifically on the transformations of systems or in systems. Social change can thus be analyzed as the product of the adjustments of the elements of the social system in relation to each other and of the adaptation of these systems to variations in its environment (2002, 15). Other researchers such as Chandessais define a system as "a structured whole whose elements vary over time. These elements are endowed with certain variable attributes and interact with each other" (Chandessais, 1994, p. 13). We believe it is important to take into consideration certain essential concepts to explain the functioning of the Haitian radio system.

First, it is the interrelationship or interaction that refers to the idea of nonlinear causality. The various actors involved in the construction of the Haitian radio system are in constant interaction. Also, the concept of an organization that makes it possible to understand the very nature of a system, the arrangement of a totality according to the structuring of its components. We say in this case that radio stations and the various components of the radio system are first and foremost a question of organization. They form a set organized in the sense that they are made up of all the Haitian radio stations and the other actors indicated above. The state of the system or its configuration is a result that is not wanted by the actors. The system is the result of the sum of everyone's actions, but no one controls this outcome. The media system is not a finalized system; it is not a system designed and built to achieve a certain result.

The Great Properties of a System

We have just presented some general definitions of the concept of system and other general considerations of the systems approach. In this section, we present the fundamental properties of any system as defined by Charron and de Bonville. Generally, a system is considered forming a whole or a totality. In their research, Charron and de Bonville take up and discuss "four properties of any system," which they say are highlighted by the definition proposed by Von Bertalanffy. They consider a system to be a totality, a regulated whole, a dynamic set, and a set of interdependent elements (2002.9). We will come back to this in much more detail. Thus, researchers present the building blocks of a system as "variables" because, they say, of their ability to accept different "states" or "values." These four properties specified by Charron, and de Bonville form the basis of our analysis. Based on their work, we develop and explain each of these four properties and then look at how they apply to the Haitian radio system.

The System as a Changing Totality

The building blocks of a system are far from isolated. They are intimately linked, interdependent, and constantly changing. The notion of totality or totality underlying system means that the whole is more than the sum of its constituent elements. Each of the elements of the system contributes to the functioning of the whole which is both harmonious and conflictual in some cases. From a systemic perspective, it is not possible to speak of news radio without the existence of an audience, without sources of information and funding, without the presence of regulatory bodies that interact. Nevertheless, there may be divergences which, for the actors, represent points of tension or sources of conflict, and which are likely to bring about change. This means that the system is a whole, certainly, but it is not perfectly coherent or static. According to Charron and de Bonville,

> Relationship systems are dynamic, moving entities; the elements (or subsystems) which compose them are in constant adjustment to each other [...]. Social change no longer appears as a rupture, but as an endless and indefinite pro-

cess of transformations. Thus society, as a whole, engaged in an uninterrupted movement of transformations, occurs and reproduces itself without ceasing; more precisely, it is the result of the systemic relationships that inhabit and define it while producing it. (2002.15)

They further argue that relationship systems are active, action entities whose constituent elements adjust to each other consistently. According to the researchers, the transformation of society should not be understood as a rupture, but rather as a process of indefinite change (Charron and de Bonville 2002,15). For some researchers such as Boilly, "a system is a set of elements in solidarity with each other and forming a whole" (2000.17). In other words, there is a connection between the different elements that make up the system. For other researchers such as Chandessais, "the elements of the whole forming a system are generally called subsystems and to the extent that they perform operations, by modifying them, variables are also called operators or transducers" (1994, 14). It is in this sense that we consider the actors of the Haitian radio system as forming a system of relations.

The System as a Regulated Whole

A system is seen as a regulated whole, which operates according to very specific rules. "A rule is a line of conduct, a principle of orientation of action, a model of behavior. The rule says what one can or should do in a particular context; it indicates what behavior is generally expected in this context" (Charron and Le Cam, 2018, p. 20). A system is at the same time a regulated, coherent, and interdependent totality. Formally or informally, the behavior of actors in a system is guided by rules because there are several principles that govern the functioning of the system or the actions of the actors who compose it. Thus, a radio system such as that of Haiti operates in accordance with several rules, for example, the principle of competition found in all media systems. This is because the actors of the system, especially the radios, are in competition with each other to appropriate the resources available in their environment. This is a principle of system regulation. "The notion of a regulatory system refers to the strategic notion of the rules of the game, the rules defining the nature of the game. In a game, the freedom of action of the players is never total; their choices are limited by a set of rules that set the framework within which these choices must be made" (Charron, 1990.81).   Radio stations as actors in the radio system act according to the principle of mimicry and distinction. This is also another form of regulation as we explain later in this section.[1]

> Every system postulate regulation, implicit or explicit, that the relations be-
> tween its parts obey sufficiently stable rules. The efforts of the parties cannot
> develop freely. They fit into a universe of rules, which means that we can find
> between them the same mechanisms of the game that we have diagnosed from
> primary power relations; not only are certain behaviors prohibited or penalized,
> but both possible maneuvers and gains and losses are if not determined at least
> defined and limited by rules, which allows everyone to perform a rational cal-
> culation and develop a strategy. (Crozier and Thoenig, 1975, 26)

In the case of Haiti, there are very few formal rules that govern the behavior of actors, particularly about competition for advertising revenues. Haitian radio stations, as is the case in other countries, have bosses, officials, and journalists who try to pull out of the game, following a certain rationality. It is a system of actors, who have a capacity for strategic action. It should be stressed that the actors are not totally constrained by the rules of the system. They have oppor-tunities for action and violation of certain rules that can also lead to changes or the negotiation of new rules. Rules guide behaviors, but do not determine them.

Nevertheless, according to Charron and de Bonville, "the rules to which ac-tors are subject is often contradictory, which forces the actor to choose those to which he will want to comply. For example, for a journalist, the pressure of the primer opposes the respect of the embargo on information" (2002, 16). The regulation of the system can be formal and informal. For example, competition between elements of the system for available resources, according to Charron and de Bonville, is a form of informal regulation that indicates the behavior to be adopted by actors. In our case study, for example, each radio station must monitor its competitor so as not to be deprived of its resources. We will return to the notion of competition much more in depth in the section 4.3.1.2. In some cases, competent authorities intervene to establish the rules of the game, as does CONATEL about the distribution of operating licenses for radio stations. According to Charron and de Bonville, the rules can also be classified, first as

---

[1]. It is a very sociologically charged concept. Nevertheless, in this study, the concept of distinction is not consid-ered from a sociological perspective as it is elaborated by the sociologist Pierre Bourdieu, (2012) in his famous book *La Distinction: Critique Sociale du Jugement* where it is treated as a theory of tastes and lifestyles. In Char-ron's sense, it is rather seen as a strategy of struggle, a competitive practice between actors in the media system by doing certain things to stand out from others.

semantic rules which refer globally to the activities of selection and interpretation of information at both the macro-structural and micro-structural level, then, the procedural rules on the way in which the professional activity takes place, and finally the normative rules that prescribe professional behavior. As we will see later in this section, there is a difference between rules that govern the media system as a whole and other rules that govern professional practices (journalism in this case) within the media system.

Mimicry and the search for differentiation, which paradoxically characterize competitive situations, are also a form of regulation, according to Charron and de Bonville (2004). Mimicry consists, for example, of a newspaper imitating to some extent another newspaper or other newspapers that are commercially successful or that manage to capture the attention of a large part of the public with its content and, as a result, attract more advertisers. By this imitation, the newspaper seeks to know a similar fate or to attract the same esteem as its competitor. Yet, in Haiti as elsewhere, we often hear some radio stations present themselves as those who do what others do not. By seeking to distinguish itself from others, a newspaper or radio station wants to be more commercially successful to increase its market value, to attract greater complicity with the other players in the system than its competitors. As Charron and de Bonville point out, « each company seeks to distinguish itself from the others by offering consumers advantages that meet what it considers to be the preferences of the target audience, in particular about the criteria of accessibility, relevance and cost, and that are at the same time specific and exclusive » (2004 285). Being in competition for the same resources necessary for its existence, each of the newspapers tries, they say, to be more competitive than the others, and for this each must distinguish itself in its offer or in its mode of operation. For Charron and de Bonville, mimicry and distinction create both a kind of cohesion and the dynamism of change in the newspaper system. "In journalism, the normative rules of rigor, objectivity, fairness, balance of points of view, quality, etc. that contribute to the definition of the role of the journalist can conflict with the pragmatic rules of efficiency, productivity, speed of execution, profitability, etc., which derive from the operating objectives of the newspaper organization" (Charron and de Bonville, 2004, 16). We see in this study that some normative rules change under the influence of certain factors.

The System as a Dynamic Whole

A system is far from fixed. It is constantly changing over time. We can think of a system as dynamic, because it is a set of elements that are constantly evolving over time. The relationship of journalists with their audience, the economic model of the media, in short, everything can be changed in the mode of operation of the media according to the evolution of the socio-economic context and the evolution of techniques. In an intervention as part of a seminar, Jean Charron (2014) considers journalism as a "contingent practice," that is, a dynamic practice, which changes over time and adapts with the social conditions of its existence. This is the case for certain literary genres such as poetry, opera, or novels. In other words, journalism is a public work that does not evolve in a vacuum. It is influenced by its environment, by the socio-political context in which it evolves.

The System as a Totality of Interdependent Elements

> The Haitian radio system must be seen as a set of elements that are interrelated. [...] [radios] form a system if the content of each [radio] is determined by the relationships (a) that a given set of information sources seek to establish (b) with a given set of (public) recipients (c) using a given set of financial and technical means (d) by complying with the psychocognitive rules of a given set of intermediaries through which messages are transmitted. More generally, [a radio] is part of a media system if the other categories of media present under the same spatio-temporal coordinates determine, at least in part, the operation and content of the [radios] present under these coordinates. (Charron and de Bonville, 2002, 18)[2]

This definition shows that there is a very close relationship between the different actors that make up a given system. It is well suited to the Haitian radio system that we analyze in this work. For the elements of a system, according to Charron and de Bonville, "are interdependent and form a dynamic whole in the sense that the elements are in relation to each other, so that the variations that act on the state of one element are likely to affect directly or indirectly the state of the other elements, leading to a change in the state of the system itself"

---

2. This is a definition that has been assigned to the log system. For the need of our work, we adapt it to the Haitian radio system that interests us.

(2002,278). According to Charron and de Bonville, the constituent elements of the system maintain mutually dependent bonds to the point that any evolution in the state of one element can produce impacts on the state of the other elements, and therefore, on the whole system. Nevertheless, according to the researchers, this interdependence between the elements of the system is relative and presents changing positions of interdependence, because the situation of a system is therefore the result of mutual accommodations between its characteristic elements.

Haitian radio stations are interdependent because, as in any system, they compete for the same available resources. The Haitian radio system can also be considered an organized system. According to (Charron & De Bonville 2002), "the notion of competition in the market qualifies the nature of relationships in the system. More precisely, it makes interdependence a fundamental attribute of the relationships between the agents who participate in the system" (2002, 279). While the system's approach can be applied to different fields, it is its application in the media field, particularly in the radio system, that interests us in this study. It is a subsystem of the Haitian media system. Other elements can also be considered as a subsystem of a given media system.

For example, Charron and de Bonville consider "journalism" as a media subsystem that is not necessarily subject to the same rules as the media system. The rules of the latter, according to the researchers, are distinct from those applicable to the production of journalistic discourse (2002.36). Jean Charron, for his part, considers journalism as a "regulated practice that consists in making a newspaper," no matter on radio and television through the editions of news commonly called, "newspaper," and in the written press, journalism remains a regulated practice. So how does this public work in its enunciation become transformed in the long term in the case of Haiti? The transformation of the Haitian radio system also implies significant changes in the rules of the operation of journalists. It is obvious that any system is governed by rules that are not static. They evolve over time. Thus, the transformation of the Haitian radio system, for example, can lead to changes in the rules of the operation of radio stations or even in the rules of the game of national political deliberation that are quite distinct from them. Charron and de Bonville (2002) consider journalism to be a discursive practice relating to public affairs (p. 142), that is, a practice of public communication. According to them, "journalism is, by definition, a realistic discursive practice, dealing with a real referent, as opposed to other modes of expression, such as literature or painting, whose referents are or can be fictitious or imaginary".[3]

The Large Dimensions of the Log System

To grasp the notion of the newspaper system, Charron and de Bonville (2002) introduce other dimensions into its definition and composition. We consider that what is said here about newspapers applies, mutatis mutandis, to radio. Researchers identify a minimum of six dimensions that they consider to be the most relevant. These are the economy, technology, sources of information, the public, the socio-cognitive system, and the content. We will summarize each of these dimensions retained by researchers and see how they apply to the Haitian radio system. If we considered the first dimension, which is economic, the researchers argue that it "refers to the overall commercial profitability of a set of newspapers and whose level influences the strategic room for maneuver of managers" (Charron and de Bonville, 2002 a, 227). Also, they see sources of income and expenditure as a subdimension of the economic dimension of the system. At this level, they say, newspapers constitute a system if, among other things: "the advertising revenues of each newspaper are a function of the advertising revenues of the other newspapers present in the same set" (227). There, we are still in a relationship of interdependence, as is the case for Haitian radio stations.[4]

The second dimension relating to the concept of a newspaper system is of a technical nature. According to the researchers, "the technical dimension concerns the material means necessary for the collection, processing, production and dissemination of information and used by a set of newspapers under common spatio-temporal coordinates" (Charron, 2014, 227). In our case study, we see how the transformation of this technical dimension influences the relations between the actors of the Haitian radio system, particularly with the digital tools that transform the means of collection, processing, and dissemination of information.

---

3. It should be noted that the use of the term "media system" can refer to different realities. For example, a researcher like Michel Mathien (1992, 1989) uses the notion of a media system to designate a particular media as forming a system. Nevertheless, in our case study, it is a set of media that forms a system of relations with other actors. This makes the syntagm media system used by Mathien the same, but there is a certain conceptual difference.

4. It is important to note that this passage refers to newspapers which, in Canada and in most countries, are private companies subject to a profitability imperative. If we want to broaden the subject to all media, including public broadcasters, we will have to add to the economic dimension the mode of ownership.

The dimension of the sources is also very important in the definition of the newspaper system and, consequently, in the radio system we analyze. Regarding this dimension, researchers shall take into consideration all naturalized or legal persons seeking to disseminate information or advertising messages in newspapers. "Sources can therefore be divided into two main sub-dimensions: sources that buy space because they are interested in the readers of the newspaper, sources to which the newspaper gives space because its readers are presumed to be interested in them" (Brin, Charron, et de Bonville 2004, 228). To the extent that the sources manage to reach their target in a suppletive and concurrent manner, the researchers then talk about the formation of a system. The public is seen as a fifth dimension that has caught the attention of researchers in defining the newspaper system. According to (Brin, Charron, et De Bonville 2004)"the public dimension of the press refers to the socio-demographic and cultural characteristics of the public that may influence the choice and reading of newspapers" (229). In this case, the authors speak of a newspaper system insofar as the arrangement of the audience of a newspaper in the system influences the composition of the audience of the other newspapers present in the same system. This is one of the fundamental dimensions of our case study. For example, if a newspaper's readership increases significantly, it is potentially to the detriment of one or more other newspapers. Another dimension mentioned by the researchers is the sociocognitive dimension, which indicates the cognitive composition present in the brains of journalists, and which allows them to carry out the various activities (collection, processing, production, and dissemination of information) that enter the daily life of journalistic work. According to the researchers, the work of journalists must meet the requirements of the newspaper hierarchy, the public, news sources, and members of the journalists' corporation. Thus, according to them, "newspapers form a system if the cognitive structures used by the journalists of one or the other of the newspapers are influenced by the way in which information is collected, processed, produced or disseminated in the other newspapers" (Brin, Charron and de Bonville, 2004, 228).

The last dimension, which is not the least, concerns the content that relates to the semantic and morphological characteristics of the editorial and advertising content of newspapers. Based on this last dimension, Charron and de Bonville identify five conditions that must be met to give rise to a newspaper system. First, the topics chosen by a newspaper that is part of the same system are influenced by topics already covered in one or other of the system's journals. Then, the contents of a specific theme treated in a newspaper produce impacts on the choice of information of the other newspapers that participate in the constitution of the whole. Then, the researchers argue that the way in which journalistic genres are defined and used by any newspaper in the system also influences the way in which these same journalistic genres are used and defined by the other newspapers that are part of the whole. And finally, the last two points concern the influence of styles, typographic, and graphic presentations used in a newspaper on the choice of another newspaper of the newspaper system. In conclusion, Brin, Charron and de Bonville (2004) point out that "the existence of a system of newspapers at the content level implies the presence of a set of rules common to journalists working in these newspapers and guiding their professional practice in the choice of events and information to be reported on these events, in stylistic choices, etc." (229).

The analysis of the dimensions relating to the concept of the log system shows that the operation of the system is based on what Charron, and de Bonville call the principle of mimicry and distinction. Because, according to them, a newspaper tends to "imitate the newspapers that seem to it to be the most commercially successful or whose content seems to be the most appreciated by the public, by sources, by the professional community, etc. with the aim of achieving the same success and/or attracting the same esteem" (230). Based on our personal experience in journalism, we can say that this is a daily practice in the newsrooms of Haitian radio stations. In each newsroom, there is a person responsible for monitoring and copying the contents of the main news editions of the dominant radio stations in Port-au-Prince. This same attitude is observed on the side of the leading opinion journalists who host public debate programs. The lesser-known ones seek to imitate those who have already made their name in the profession and who manage to capture the attention of a large part of the local population and the diaspora. Those who are at the same level rather seek to distinguish themselves as is the case for the star journalist of Radio Vision 2000, Valéry Numa, who sometimes neglects the burning political files echoing in other radio stations to deal with much more social subjects, or the discovery and promotion of new talents who achieve extraordinary things.

The Place of Journalism in the Media System

What is the place of journalism in the media system, particularly radio? What is likely to change in Haitian journalistic practices depending on the factors to explain the transformation of the system? There can be no journalism without a technical infrastructure of broadcasting which is the media. Brin, Charron and de Bonville (2004) consider journalism as "a set of rules allowing the reproduction of a specific discursive practice" (70). According to Brin, Charron and de Bonville (2004), "journalism forms a set of contingent discursive practices. In other words, there is no reality, identical always and in all countries, that would be referred to by the word journalism. On the contrary, journalism is a socio-cultural construct strongly marked by the context of its formulation" (88). As far as we are concerned, it is obvious that journalistic practices change under the influence of several factors as we see in our analysis. What is the place of journalism in the Haitian radio system that we describe in particular? Are journalists subject to the same rules as before?

Journalism as a Regulated Practice

Changes in the relationships between the actors of a given media system necessarily imply changes in the regulation of journalistic practices. In systemic logic, journalism appears as a regulated practice in the sense that it obeys rules and is part of a system of relations with a discursive aim. Based on this attribute of journalism, according to Charron, a citizen can recognize a newspaper article because of its structure and content. Journalistic work obeys basic principles such as objectivity, impartiality, neutrality, verification of sources of information. The application of the rules is systemic in nature because it concerns many agents, spread over a relatively large space-time (Charron 2016).

According to Brin, Charron and de Bonville (2004), the rules themselves constitute a homogeneous and drastic normative system. They are characteristic of what they call the journalistic paradigm. This means that the transformation of a radio system necessarily leads to changes in the rules of the operation of journalism in Haiti. Being a subsystem in the media system, journalists, according to Charron, collectively establish a normative framework that governs the functioning of the journalist community. The rules that structure professional practice are subject to appropriation, but also to transformation. Their use by a community of journalists induces an uninterrupted process of adjustment, adaptation, innovation, the consequence of which is that the reproduction of the rules established by journalists is at the same time the production of new rules (Brin, Charron and de Bonville, 2 004 224–225). The development and application of a code of professional ethics, for example.

A Competitive Relationship Between Actors for Available Resources

Competition remains one of the key factors in the transformation of the Haitian radio system. This competition, as Brin Charron and de Bonville (2004) point out, takes place in a multiple market. Because they consider that competition between journalists and companies takes place in at least five distinct markets: "the market for consumers of information, the market for advertisers, the market for sources of information, the market for investors and finally the market for prestige and professional recognition" (281). In the context of the development of digital technologies, we see that there are fewer and fewer boundaries between the function of each of the actors in the system. It is for this reason that we evoke the thesis of a generalization of competition between the main players in the system. And, in this widespread competition, it seems to us that the traditional media are the main losers. Media managers often claim that their main activity is to sell journalistic information or content to the public. However, according to Brin Charron and de Bonville (2004), "more often than not, this claim does not correspond to reality, since most media companies derive most, sometimes all, of their revenues from advertising" (281). This is practically the case in Haiti. The activity of radio stations is rather to capture the attention of the public and then resell it to advertisers. Everyone remembers that famous statement by a TF1 director, Patrick Le Lay, who said: "There are many ways to talk about television, but from a business perspective, let's be realistic. Basically, TF1's job is to help a brand sell its product... However, for an advertising message to be perceived, the viewer's brain must be available. Our programs are intended to make it available, to entertain it, to relax it to prepare it between two messages. What we sell to brands is available human brain time" (Lancien 2005). This statement sparked a wave of reactions, but many critics thought it was rather honest. In the case of the written press, the person in charge may claim to sell newspapers to consumers, but in the case of radio, those responsible cannot make that claim. Never in the history of radio in Haiti have listeners paid any fees to access radio content. The only counterpart of the listeners is the time they devote to listening to the radio. As Brin, Charron and de Bonville (2004) pointed out, "advertising financing therefore places media companies in competition in two markets at once: they compete for consumer attention and advertisers' advertising budgets" (81). According to our definition, the Haitian radio system is characterized by competition between the different actors of the system to monopolize the attention of the public. The different actors are in constant interaction and in a relationship of interdependence. Public attention is the main issue in this competition. Brin, Charron and de Bonville (2004) describe the interplay of media competition in the advertising market from the late nineteenth century to 2004. We used this description to explain this game of competition between the actors of the Haitian radio system.

According to their main hypothesis, Brin, Charron and de Bonville (2004), suggest that "the economic and technical conditions prevailing in the contemporary media system led to a shift in the center of gravity of the competitive game between media companies and journalists" (276). Based on the intensity of rivalry in the media system and considering the technical modalities in which it is exercised, the researchers argue that journalism that has been practiced in a competitive situation is gradually subject to a competitive regime that is close to the theoretical model of hyper-competition (290).

Our work is also an extension of this work. The notion of hyper-competition also has a qualitative dimension, i.e., competition changes in nature. In a regime of media competition, competition for public attention is primarily the responsibility of those responsible for the media and commercial services. In a regime of hyper competition, the producers of the messages (journalists) become conscious and anxious actors to participate in a competition for attention and they produce their messages accordingly. The "wall" that once separated editorial from commercial services is disappearing.

In this case, this hyper-competition is explained by a growing increase in the number of radio stations an intensification of the radio offer, a scattering of the public, the possibility for each of the actors in the system to be a media to be able to select, process and disseminate information to a specific audience. In a comparison between the situation in the 2000s and the late nineteenth century, Brin, Charron and de Bonville distinguish between media competition in three main respects. First, they cite the increase in the demand for the consumer's attention by an information offer that reached a volume and diversity unimaginable at the end of the nineteenth century. Secondly, they point out that the technical methods of receiving messages lead to a volatility of public attention. And finally, they state that journalists can know in real time how their competitors are covering events.

According to Brin, Charron and de Bonville (2004), "the fragmentation of attention through the growth of supply limits the possibility of the media to attract large audiences, while the technical conditions for capturing attention become more restrictive for them as soon as the consumer's attention can escape them at any time" (p.280)). Indeed, in our case study, the number of radio stations continues to multiply in Haiti. Yet, with digital technologies, public attention may become increasingly difficult to capture. Social media is becoming new competitors for traditional media, as we have already explained. "In a competitive market, the ability of information offers to capture and retain the attention of consumers depends on the technical and economic factors that determine the accessibility and availability of the offer" (Brin, Charron and de Bonville, 2 004 284). They see a strong growth in the number of players in the media system competing for consumer attention.

Indeed, they suggest that advertising spending is not decreasing. On the contrary, it is increasing, but not at the same rate as the (exponential) increase in the supply of advertising space. According to the researchers, there is no increase in the volume of attention available and advertising spending during this period. This observation reflects the Haitian reality. The FM band is 100% saturated in several parts of the country, as pointed out by the director of CONATEL. There are more than 700 radio stations (legal and illegal) for a population of about 10 million inhabitants, so the economic situation of the country is deteriorating day by day. To explain this intensification of competition, the researchers evoke two phenomena, which, according to them, play together. These include a congestion of the system resulting from the increase in media content (Brin, Charron and de Bonville, 2004, 290).

The fact that all actors in the system seek to monopolize the same resource, or the public's attention in "quantity and quality," contributes to the regulation of the system. In short, competition sets the rules of the game. In this system of relationships, each actor struggles for his or her own interests, for his or her own survival. In the logic of the audience, radios seek to capture the attention of a wider audience to attract a greater number of advertisers. To achieve this, they must engage in a struggle for influence to access the best sources of information or exclusive information. All this also requires human resources, qualified journalists to go in search of information. In a country where there is no higher-level journalism school, qualified journalists are also scarce resources for which the media must fight. But we see that the precariousness of Haitian radio stations does not allow them to keep the most qualified journalists for lack of economic means.

The sources of information are particularly official sources of the government, Parliament, trade unions, and the private business sector. This means that the sources of information themselves are also in a competition for access to public radio space, to intervene in prime-time radio stations to capture the attention of the public, either to sell political programs, defend themselves against accusations of opponents, defend a cause, denounce the public authorities, and/or influence public opinion in one direction or another. For their part, the interest of advertisers is to make their product known or sell to the public. To capture the public's attention, they must use radio stations to broadcast their advertising messages. What is the public interest in this competitive game? The public also needs the media to be informed and to form an opinion about a given subject, to choose its representatives, to choose its consumer products, to express points of view. In this relationship of interdependence, CONATEL as a regulatory body also has a major role to play in setting or enforcing certain rules.

The Strategic Nature of the Relations of the Actors in the Haitian Radio System

The relations between the actors of the Haitian media system must be considered from a systemic perspective. To better understand the relations between the various actors in the system, the use of the strategic approach also seems to us to be fundamental. In the sense of Crozier and Freiberg, change must be seen as a fundamentally systemic phenomenon. Like any system of relations, the Haitian radio system is open to change, or, more precisely, to the transformation of the relations of radio stations with each other, radios with sources of information, with advertisers, with the public, and with other actors who participate in the formation of the system. The strategic approach is a paradigm that is intimately linked to the theory of organizations. It is part of a broader methodological trend called methodological individualism. Strategic analysis is, in fact, an approach that was proposed by sociologists Michel Crozier and Erhard Frieberg with the publication of their book entitled, The Actor and the System, published in 1977. This book is a summary of the main theories relating to strategic analysis. In the sense of Crozier and Frieberg, strategic analysis considers that the actions of individuals are the result of a strategic choice, therefore rational, by which the actor seeks to pull out in a constraining context. "As in any complex system, no decision by any actor can be taken unilaterally; reaching an acceptable compromise is an indispensable prerequisite for any action. The special feature of this system is that a compromise is never negotiated directly between the parties directly concerned" (Crozier and Thoenig, 1975, 7). In our analysis, we consider the strategic nature of the relations between the actors of the Haitian radio system.

A Hypothetical-Inductive Approach

The strategic analysis is part of a hypothetical-inductive approach that takes the actor as a starting point to arrive at the system. The systemic approach is therefore hypothetical-deductive, which goes from the general to the specific, from the system to arrive at the actor. The two approaches are far from being in opposition. They complement each other. The strategic approach takes account of the lived experience of the actors. That is exactly what our study is about. We see in our methodological framework that our respondents are supposed to be people experienced in their respective fields. This hypothetical-inductive approach proceeds in stages to facilitate the understanding of the collective organization and the interpretation of the relations between the actors in any situation. This theoretical model allows us to conceptualize the action of the different actors within the Haitian radio system. In our case study, the actors' game can be considered as a system of concrete action, that is to say "a structured human whole that coordinates the actions of its participants in relatively stable game mechanisms and maintains its composition, that is to say the stability of its games and the relationships between them, by regulatory mechanisms that constitute other games" (Crozier and Friedberg, 2014, 286). To better understand the conjugation of the actors' game in a concrete system, Crozier and Friedberg propose to proceed both by a strategic reasoning that makes it possible to go through the actor to discover the system and by systemic reasoning that aims to highlight the order to derive from the system. Therefore, both systemic and strategic approaches are fundamental to analyzing changes in relations between the main actors of the Haitian radio system.

Charron (1990) considers the strategic systems approach as a break with traditional research habits because of its various particularities. According to him, this approach is based on a game of oscillation between observation and the development of hypotheses. It is based particularly on an ethno-methodological approach. According to Charron, the strategic approach is not necessarily an inductive approach in the narrow sense of the word. Certainly, the researcher makes empirical observations even before proceeding to the development of the theories. Nevertheless, according to Charron, in the initial stages of his approach, the researcher is guided by a certain deductive logic: "Theory, hypothesis, observation." This means that hypotheses do not fall from the sky or magically come from observation. "The difference lies in the fact that the initial hypotheses are only general and provisional and do not strictly speaking constitute research hypotheses; they are there only to guide the observation without being strictly limited" (Charron, 1990, 105). To this end, the open hypotheses formulated by the researcher are called upon to be modified throughout the research while keeping a watchful eye on his or her field of observation.

In his doctoral thesis, Charron (1990), adopts a strategic systemic approach that allowed him to build a very solid argumentation and to mobilize a set of concepts (system, environment, game, rules, strategy, negotiation, resources, constraints, power, etc.) to analyze the relations between parliamentary court-makers and political authorities. Nevertheless, he does not consider this approach to be a theory or as theoretical proposals for formulating working hypotheses. For him, the strategic systemic approach is carried out through "trial and error." It is based on consecutive experiments of explanation, predictions, and clarifications, continuously reviewed, and corrected according to observations. According to him, this approach seeks to achieve a "saturation of hypotheses" that are clarified throughout the progression of the approach.

The goal of the approach is to rebuild the game; observing the behavior of actors and measuring attitudes are the way to achieve this. From the first observational data on the strategies of the actors (and the existing work on the subject, it goes without saying), the researcher formulates hypotheses on the nature and rules of the game, s/he deduces forecasts as to the strategic behavior of the actors. These forecasts are confronted with the facts and the discrepancy that the researcher observes between his or her forecasts and the course of things leads him or her to review his or her assumptions on the nature of the game and which reflect the behavior of the actors (Charron, 1990, 104).

As is the case in this study, we have formulated a set of working hypotheses on changes in the relations between actors in the Haitian radio system who have provisional status. It is a guide that helps us in the realization of empirical data collections. Throughout this work, assumptions are constantly changing. The strategic approach is based on the premise that any system is built and regulated by establishing power relations between its adherents and between its constituent elements. According to the authors, from a sociological point of view, the essence of the characteristic features of a system lies in the methods of regulation implemented and which compose it as a system. Actors are endowed with a capacity to act individually or collectively according to their resources.

The Power Play Between the Actors of the System

Any organized action, any system of concrete relations like the Haitian radio system implies a power play between the actors who compose it. In the logic of Crozier and Friedberg (1977), power is never total. It is also limited by rules that limit the actions of actors. In a system, each of the actors defines a certain number of objectives and strategies around a power or competition game to monopolize available resources. As we have explained, each actor in a system, regardless of their place in the system, holds a certain power as a determining factor in action. In the radio system, power is shared between radio stations, advertisers, the public, regulators, and news sources. They are in a situation of interdependence and reciprocal influence.

In the sense of Crozier and Friedberg, power should not be seen as a peculiarity of an actor or actors in each system. Rather, it is a relationship of reciprocity and compromise that is done with a specific objective. This power relationship is not always balanced since the actors do not always do well in the same way. There is most often an actor who, depending on his or her advantages, fares better than the other who is not in a situation of total vulnerability (Crozier and Friedberg, 1977, 60–61). Actors do not always face the same spatio-temporal constraints. Some may find themselves in more advantageous situations, in a situation of strength or control of power. The notion of the system is also part of a constructivist perspective.

In a system, it is necessary to seek above all to determine the way in which collective actions are built based on the behavior and on the specific interests of the actors who may be opposed. Because, according to Crozier and Friedberg, the actors' game cannot always be determined by the coherence of the system in which they engage. Each actor in a system, depending on the place s/he occupies in it, holds a certain power as a determining factor of action. The power it can exercise (rather than "hold") is a function of the position it occupies, a position that allows it to mobilize certain resources. Also, power can be thought of as the ability of an actor or group of actors to influence another actor or a given group of actors, to act on their behavior or to get them to adhere to a certain vision. As Charron (1990) points out, there are some main ideas that flow from the notion of the system of action, including the interdependence of the actors and the notion of regulation, which is also a very important aspect in a system of action.

The Freedom and Rationality of the Power of the Actors in the System

The power relations and strategies of the actors in the system are at the heart of strategic analysis. According to Crozier, power implies a certain rationality. There is no real correspondence between the rationality of the individual and that of the group s/he represents. The author highlights a set of problems relating to the very structure of the system. It is above all the problem of rationality that grants the individual greater freedom in relation to his or her function in the system. Actors enjoy spaces of relative freedom from areas of uncertainty. "The rationality of the individual does not necessarily correspond to the rationality of the group he represents. Not only does the individual have as many possible strategies in the game within which he operates, but he operates in several games and can anticipate changing the main game" (Crozier and Friedberg, 1977, 27). It results from the nontaxable nature and freedom of action of the actors (408). The second problem identified by the authors is "that of the necessary lack of homology between the games that we discover at the operational levels and the game that constitutes the regulation of the system. The temptation is great indeed to extrapolate from the repetition of the same games at the base, a model of general regulation of the whole" (27). In the sense of Crozier and Friedberg, the actor's vision or objectives are not always defined precisely and coherently. They are bound to be constantly modified according to the circumstances and the results obtained. Consciously or unconsciously, the actor implements certain strategies to achieve his or her goals even while being inactive. In each system, the logical reasoning of the actors is incorporated into self-regulatory mechanisms. "The actor does not exist outside the system that defines the freedom that is his and the rationality that he can use in his action. But the system exists only by the actor who alone can carry it and give it life and who alone can change it" (Crozier and Friedberg 1977, 11). It considers the organization of common interventions as a social construct.

The Limits of Strategic Analysis

It is important to note that the strategic approach poses several challenges for researchers. According to Charron (1990), this theoretical approach puts the researcher in an epistemological embarrassment. Because, according to him, "strategic analysis pays particular attention to the experience of the actors. The game exists only through the subjectivity of the actors; this subjectivity is at the center of the 'objective' reality studied by the researcher" (Charron 1990, 105). This presupposes a double point of view of the researcher on the reality he observes. He must try to understand them by putting himself in the place of the actors, by looking at things from their point of view. But at the same time, he must keep the external gaze of the researcher and maintain his external vision as a researcher. It is, according to Charron, a question of "developing a position of exteriority which, alone, allows him to go beyond this subjective point of view and to take a critical look at the evidence and on the categories of common sense. The back and forth between the observation and the elaboration of hypotheses is therefore coupled with a back and forth between the subjectivity of the actors and the researcher's point of view of exteriority" (p. 105). It calls on the vigilance and conscience of the researcher to avoid any confusion relating to the two points of view. In particular, the researcher must avoid giving the commonsense explanations provided by the actors. "The strategic approach is concerned with adjusting the means available to actors for the purposes they pursue" (Charron, 1990.80). Because the formal structure of the system does not definitively determine the attitude of the actors. Rather, it is the result of a rational approach to action within the obligations required by the system. It is a sociological approach that is based on reasoning, tangible decision-making by actors within the environment in which they evolve.

Partial Conclusion

From all the above, we deduce a very close relationship between the different constituent elements of our conceptual framework. The system remains a fundamental concept to analyze our case study. In particular, the changes in the relations between the different actors of the Haitian radio system under the influence of several factors specified in our general problem. Despite its theoretical depth, this approach remains insufficient to analyze all aspects of our case study. This leads us to make use of other theoretical concepts such as the notion of public space in a more contemporary perspective to analyze the participation of the Haitian public in radio debate programs. Since Haitians in the diaspora are an important component of the Haitian public, we saw fit to introduce the notion of transnationalism to analyze this component of the Haitian public in the national political deliberation. As in any communication situation, there are rules that govern the exchanges that take place in the Haitian radio space between the different exchange partners. That is why we also give pride of place to the concept of a public communication contract. These are four pillars of our theoretical and conceptual framework. A large part of the proposals presented in this study are changes that began since the introduction of Creole in radio that continued after the fall of the Duvalier dictatorship but accelerated with the development and use of digital tools by the actors of the system.

The Distinctive Features of Contemporary Public Space

The change in the relations between the actors of the Haitian radio system, especially between journalists and the radio audience, is a fundamental element of our study. The new forms of reception of information and participation of the Haitian public in radio talk shows is the subject of a very in-depth analysis in this study. To analyze this aspect, we have seen fit to introduce into our theoretical framework another fundamental concept or another theoretical approach which is the public space despite the depth and richness of the systemic approach mentioned above. The concept of public space is very important for understanding and analyzing the participation of the Haitian public in radio public debate broadcasts. This is because the transformation of the Haitian radio space also leads to changes in the modalities of participation of the actors of the Haitian public space in public debates and the rules of the game of national political deliberation.

The Haitian public space refers to all the places where public debates take place on the Haitian national territory. These are the debates that take place largely on the radio and in other media, but also in the Haitian parliament, in municipal councils, in citizens' associations, in street demonstrations, in public squares, in café terraces, and in universities. One of the peculiarities of the Haitian public space is that a large part of this audience is outside the borders of Haiti, but this diasporic audience listens to the programs and participates in the programs of the radio stations that broadcast from Port-au-Prince. The participation of this component of the Haitian public is analyzed in this study in a specific way.

In this work, we have chosen not to return to the philosophical and normative conception of public space developed by the German philosopher Jugen Habermas (1988). To analyze the changes in the relations between the Haitian public and the media, particularly its participation in public debates, we introduce a much more contemporary approach to the notion of public space (Miège, 2010). The various criticisms addressed to Habermas's work do not necessarily call into question the originality and importance of his theses; rather, they point to a certain ambiguity that overlays his theses. The work of the latter is therefore simply overtaken by the realities of contemporary public space. In the current context of the development of digital technologies, public space is characterized by very specific features. In the sense that "contemporary public space is shaped by new historical forces; it may have new potential. To the extent that we are concerned with democratic dynamism, the development of a theory of public space, adapted to contemporary facts, is essential for research-ers as well as political actors" (Fraser 2005, Dahlgren et al., 1994, 244)." As an alternative to Habermassian normative theory, many new approaches have been developed in recent decades.

The idea of a global or transnational public space began to make its way into the world of social science research decades ago. Through a very in-depth analysis, Dahlgren and Rilieu (2000) highlight some features that explain the functioning of public space on the internet. They highlight three analytical di-mensions of contemporary public space considered to be three main elements inseparable from the perspective of the public sphere: it is a structural level, a spatial level, and a communicational level. These three dimensions, according to them, constitute an analytical starting point for examining the public sphere of a given society or analyzing the contribution of any communication tech-nology. The structural dimension refers, on the one hand, to the characteristics of the media system, including universal access and, on the other hand, to the social and political structures of society. It is characterized, according to the authors, particularly by the idea of universality on which the notion of public space is based, a space open to all and which does not make any exclusion. "While the media are the major feature of public space, it follows normatively that they should remain technically, economically, culturally, and linguistically within the reach of members of society; the a priori exclusion of any segment of the population contradicts democracy claims to universalism" (Dahlgren and Rilieu 2000, 163). Universalism, in our opinion, will always remain an ideal to be achieved, a utopia in this context.

In addition to the structural dimension, two other dimensions are put forward by Dahlgren and Rilieu (2000). According to them, there is the spatial dimen-sion or "spatial boundary" which is explained above all by the permeability of contemporary public space, which is no longer confined within a nation-state, but which goes beyond the framework of inter-state borders. It is in this sense that the Haitian diaspora that is outside Haitian borders are considered part of the Haitian internal public space. In the modern world, mass media and inter-active media such as the NET play a very important role in the constitution of space" (Dahlgren and Rilieu, 2000,166). About the communicational dimen-sion or "communicational action," "the public space is seen as the discursive negotiation of norms and values based on linguistic and cultural intersubjectivi-ty and competence." These three dimensions of public space are very important for our work. First, on a structural level, digital technologies are likely to lead to major changes in the power relations between the various actors involved in the Haitian public space. Then, on the spatial level, it seems obvious to us that the public space we are studying connects a national audience and a transna-tional public that addresses the same nation-state. The public radio space we are studying goes beyond Haitian borders. And finally, we study the Haitian public radio space, as a concrete space for communication and contradictory debates in which local Haitian actors and the diaspora participate. As we have already pointed out, the Haitian public space is largely limited to the media space, dom-inated by the radio space that we study more specifically. It is according to these characteristics that Dahlgren studies the internet as a tool that promotes reterri-torialized or transnational exchanges or communication practices.

Given its communicative potential in its current phase of development, Dahl-gren and Rilieu (2000) consider the internet to be "a multimodal medium," an extension of the original logic of traditional mass media. "Online versions of televisions, broadcasting stations, news agencies and daily newspapers repre-sent a considerable part of the activity of the net, while many traditional mass media now have an online presence (Dahlgren and Rilieu, 2000, 172). This multi-modality of the internet, according to the researchers, is particularly re-flected in the possibility of a single individual to address many other people simultaneously (one-to-many). But also, it allows a multitude of users to ad-dress a plurality of consumers. This is the case, for example, for Usenet forums and spaces dedicated to online discussion. 'Embodying the virtues of a pole of expansion, the net reinforces the plural character of public space. The Net pro-duces a myriad of specialized mini-public spaces and alternative public spaces. Even if some are racist and neo-fascist, the whole presents a positive balance for democracy' (Dahlgren and Rilieu, 2000, 176).

Other researchers such as (Rasmussen 2014) approach the complexity of contemporary public sphere theory about the media and the internet as a new platform for public debate. 'The concept of the public sphere represents one of the most powerful theoretical junctions between media studies and political sociology. It provides political media studies with a broader theoretical frame-work that connects the media to democracy and legitimacy of politics, and it specifies how democracy works or doesn't work in practice' (Rasmussen, 2014, 1315). We can even say that the concept of public space is one of the most mo-bilized concepts in social science studies since its theorization by Habermas. Nevertheless, studies on the function of the internet in the transformation of public spaces give rise to different perspectives.

Internet and Public Space: Different Perspectives

According to Dahlgren, research into the role of the internet in the public sphere leads to two competing perspectives. There is, according to him, a first point of view that underlies that the contribution of the ito the transformation of delib-erative democracy is still modest. To make this demonstration, he relied partic-ularly on the work of Margolis and Resnick (2000) who consider, for example, political life on the Net as being only a reinforcement of offline political life. They are particularly working on how the internet affects American political life. The argument made by these researchers in question, according to Dahl-gren, is that the use of digital technologies in the political world does not nec-essarily lead to greater citizen participation in democratic life or to a profound change in the way politics is done. The solution to this problem, according to Dahlgren, must lie in a revival of classical models of political participation and modes of political communication (156).

As Mabi and Théviot (2014) observe, 'the proliferation of participatory mech-anisms mobilizing digital tools has quickly aroused the interest of researchers, producing an important literature dealing with the relationship between the Web and politics, particularly in terms of citizen participation' (8). In their re-view of the literature, they highlight three contradictory theses. First of all, it is the 'standardization thesis' developed by some researchers such as Margolis and Resnick (2000) who defend the idea that people who are active online are those who were already offline (8). This would mean that diaspora individuals who did not have a motivation for offline political participation will still not be interested in online political content relating to their country of origin. Then, they highlight the 'thesis of mobilization' which was based on the function of the internet in mobilizing new audiences and thus supported the involvement of citizens in political life. This is the idea that the internet gives the oppor-tunity to attract new audiences. According to the authors, 'proponents of this thesis are likely to foster interactions between rulers and the governed, in the sense that the governed can speak online and make criticisms or suggestions' (9). And finally, they evoke the 'thesis of differentiation' according to which the socio-demographic particularities of the user, the orientations of technical tools, etc., are the main factors of variation of participatory users online." To this end, we can deduce that people in the diaspora who participate in the public debate of their country of origin via digital technologies are those who used to do so offline before migrating and who continue to participate in active (offline) political life in their host country.

In another article, Dahlgren (2015) makes a very constructive critique of Volkmer's book (2014) in which he suggests a new "contemporary structural transformation" of the public sphere with a new conceptual profile. This transformation of public space can be explained by three factors. First, there is what Volkmer calls "familiar and technical communication macro-networks—with their active user audiences" that are a harbinger for "contemporary global communication." It highlights the "multi-level" nature of the media and their modes of communication. Next, Dahlgren points out that the "new global sphere" lies in "the communication—and editing, mixing, filtering, and editing—of content." And finally, the public sphere, according to the author, is shaped by individualized nodes that are in a particular structural whole that connects individuals across all countries of the world (1423). "We have thereby left behind the defining framework of nation states, and moved to a regime where the local blends readily with the global and all stops in between, based on the identities, loyalties, and allegiances of the actors, operating across the full range of media technologies and platforms; this global public sphere operates across supra- and subnational societal contexts" (Dahlgren, 2015.1424)." Is it possible to reconcile traditional models with new forms of political participation? Because cyberspace plays a leading role in the current political mobilizations as we have seen during some presidential election campaigns such as that of Barak Obama and Donald Trump. Some researchers see the internet as a factor in the disorganization of public space and the destruction of traditional media. (Leterre 2010) goes so far as to say that "the Internet participates strongly in the deinstitutionalization of exchange, in the absence of collective rules, in collective consequences—such as deliberation in a democratic regime." Throughout his text, he defends the thesis of a disarticulation of the concepts of individual and collectivity in different computer networks.

Other researchers abound differently. In a study of online deliberative democracy, (Dahlberg 2001) examines how it operates through cyberspace. To achieve this, he makes use of a comparative analysis of online discourse based on the requirements of the public sphere stemming from Habermas normative philosophy. At the end of his study, he concludes that the expansion of the public sphere through the internet gives rise, at the same time, to the growth of deliberative spaces and to the participation of citizens in public delibera- tion. For his part, Castells (2009) presents a vast theory of urban planning in the information age based on the differentiation between the space of places and the space of flows. In his approach, he makes it clear that space is far from being a patent reality. It highlights the economic and social transformation of the information age and shows how what he calls "the networked society" is being fully strengthened on a global scale. It places particular emphasis on the impact of the information age on all aspects of society. Castells' approach is joined in part by a researcher like Campbell (2013) who takes a critical look at the notion of the public sphere from a contemporary perspective. Van Den Bos and Nell (2006) agree, but with some nuances. They review the transna- tional nature of new media and their use by Iranian and Turkish Kurdish mi- grants in the Netherlands. "The territoriality in Iranian and Turkish—Kurdish online interaction in the Netherlands underlines our view of virtual space as anchored in offline contexts rather than as a self-contained, disembodied uni- verse p.35)." They found some variation in territoriality in online interaction across geographic scale.

An Analysis from the Point of View of the Public Communication Contract

Any communication situation is governed by norms that guide the behavior or actions of the interlocutors. The Haitian radio system is above all a system of social relations as we have just seen. This implies that the relations between the different actors of the system are governed by a set of communicational rules, conventions, and reciprocal expectations that Charron and Le Cam (2008) call a *public communication contract*. For us, this is a very important concept for analyzing changes in the relations between the different actors of the Haitian radio system. In this study, the idea of a communication contract brings us back to the fundamental role that radio claims to play in its relations with its audience through participation in its debate shows and in its relations with other actors in the system.

We place particular emphasis on the relationship of radio stations and journalists with their audience. Journalists play both an information role and an
animation of public debate through a confrontation of points of view between
communication partners. Thus, there are modalities, rules that govern the participation of the public in radio debates, including the hosts always take the
time to remind the participants from the beginning of the show. The communication contract is understood as "a framework of recognition to which the partners subscribe so that exchange and intercom prehension can be established"
(Charaudeau, 1993, 6). According to the linguist, a communication contract
is never irrevocable and fixed. It can be renegotiated, updated by the various
exchange partners. That is, "in public communication, clauses are not defined
once and for all. They are likely to change through the moves that players play.
The negotiation is never over; the contract is never definitively ratified" (Charron and Le Cam, 2018, 25). They see negotiation and accession as ongoing
processes. Any communication situation, according to Charaudeau (1997), defines a frame of reference that generates the modalities of exchange between
protagonists. In Charaudeau's sense, the terms of the contract can be renegotiated, redefined, or updated by stakeholders depending on the circumstances.
Charron and Le Cam agree, because, according to them, "in public communication, clauses are not defined once and for all. They are likely to change
through the moves that players play. The negotiation is never over; the contract
is never definitively ratified" (Charron and Le Cam, 2018, 25). Thus, they see
negotiation and consent as uninterrupted or ongoing processes between communication partners.

According to Charaudeau (1993), the conditions of communication are based
on four principles inseparable from each other. It is first a principle of interaction defining the communication operation as a manifestation of exchange
between two actors (p. 2). Then, there is a principle of relevance that is based
on "shared knowledge" without which comprehension between communication partners would be impossible. Then there is the principle of influence according to which any communication action is a competition to control the
stakes of communication. And finally, there is "a principle of regulation that
determines, at the same time, the conditions for the partners of communication to come into contact and recognize themselves as legitimized partners,
and the conditions for the continuation and completion of the communicative
exchange" (Charaudeau, 1993.5). This last principle is of particular interest to
us in this work. Charaudeau defines any act of language as "an act of interac-

tional exchange between two partners (communicating subject and interpreting subject) bound by a principle of intentionality, this exchange always occurring in a certain situation of communication" (Charaudeau 2006, 1). As in other media systems, the confrontation of different types of discourse circulating in the Haitian radio space is governed by a set of rules that may be different depending on the nature or discursive aim of the interventions (Charaudeau, Maingueneau, and Adam, 2002).

According to Charaudeau, "the situation of communication constitutes the frame of reference to which individuals in a social community are attached when they enter into communication" (Charaudeau, 1997, 67). This frame of reference allows interlocutors to influence each other, to attack each other, to seduce each other, to value their acts of language, and to build meaning (Charaudeau, 1997). Any situation of communication or interaction brings together two people whom Charaudeau calls, in a definition of the act of language, partners. Charaudeau compares the communication situation to a theater stage because of the constraints of space, time, relationships, and words to which the interlocutors are subjected. In radio talk shows, for example, it is up to the hosts to remind guests of the rules of language behavior or the need to submit to the constraints relating to the communication situation that apply to all interlocutors without distinction. Charaudeau asserts that it is the situation of communication that gives meaning to the act of communication. We see that in the communication contract, the animators commit to finding guests who can help the audience understand the events that marked the news of the week. Nevertheless, they are also committed to giving the public the latest news in their immediacy that has a public interest. It is perhaps with this in mind that the hosts accept some accidental or unsolicited participation from the public, as we see in our analysis.

The Purpose of a Radio Communication Contract

In a radio program, the hosts personify the radio stations for which they work. They are called upon to ensure compliance with the terms of the communication contract that binds the station, in general, and more specifically, the program, with its audience. What is the purpose of a communication contract in a radio talk show? Charaudeau highlights a tension between two opposing aims relating to the dual purpose of the media contract: those of information and capture. According to him, the informational aim is to make citizens aware of everything that has happened or what is happening in the world and that is worthy of their interest. Thus, the media body implements two kinds of language activities to achieve this informational aim. It is, on the one hand, the description that consists of reporting current events, events that have occurred throughout the world in their instantaneity. For example, what news radio stations do daily through news editions, newsletters, and news flashes reflect this description well. This is part of the communication contract that connects news radio stations with their audience. And on the other hand, the second language activity implemented by the media body is that of explanation whose purpose is to enlighten the public on the causes and consequences of the facts reported. This is precisely what the hosts of the programs seek to do by inviting personalities to comment on current events, as we see in Chapter Five in our typology of forms of participation in radio debate programs. The second aim is that of "capture." The media body must make every effort to capture and retain the attention of the public. According to Charaudeau, in this respect nothing is taken for granted in advance for the media which are in a situation of competition for attention available.[5]

The Impact of Digital Technology in Traditional Media Spaces

Researchers are almost unanimous in recognizing that digital technologies exert a very strong influence on the composition of public spaces. Nevertheless, opinions are divided on the effects of the internet on public spaces and traditional media. One of the consequences of digital technologies is the blurring of boundaries between diasporic communities and their countries of origin. The media allow migrants to be as close as possible to their country of origin.

The amount of research done over the past two decades on the relationship between the diaspora, the internet and public spaces is growing. Nevertheless, Parham (2005) believes that the development of public sphere theory dealing with the complexity and new challenges of the world, facilitated by the internet, is still at the outset stage (375). So we can say that the development of digital technologies continues to surprise us, to transform our daily lives. As Dahlgren and Rilieu (2000) have found so well:

---

5. Charaudeau, Patrick. *The Discourse of Media Information: The Construction of the Social Mirror.* Media-Research Collection. Paris: Nathan; Institut National de l'audiovisuel, 1997, p 2–5.

> The Internet promises and gives a lot. It can strengthen, expand our worlds, offer huge streams of information, help us connect with people who share our interests. It can distract us, provoke us, or tempt us. It can also absorb us, engulf us, and immerse us in a volume of information that we can never use. It can promote our consumerist identities, but also, with some effort on our part, allow us to cultivate our civic identities. Does the net help us build a better democracy? The net has the capacity to expand public space, although it does not seem to dramatically transform political life. (183)

The internet, like science and technology, has its advantages and disadvantages. We believe that the analysis of Dahlgren and Rilieu (2000) summarizes well the potentialities of the internet or the double face of technological tools.

The Relations of Haitians in the Diaspora with the Media of Their Country of Origin: A Transnational Approach to International Migration

We consider the participation of the Haitian diaspora in the national public debate through digital technologies to be one of the key factors participating in this transformation of the Haitian media environment. In our introduction, we gave an operational definition of the concept of Haitian diaspora. In the scientific literature, several definitions of the concept of diaspora are proposed. "We can define the diaspora as a social construction aimed at establishing and maintaining links between migrant populations who believe they come from the same origin, real or mythical, thus having their own characteristics that separate them from host societies" (Bruneau 2004, 24). This definition corresponds well to our research concern because the Haitian diaspora, as we had already defined, refers to all the realities it describes. That is to say, "the presence of populations with the same geographical, national, and religious references in different national spaces has given rise to the development of the concept of diaspora" (Kastoryano 2013, 90.) The notion of the diaspora is used to describe many distinct phenomena. This is also the observation of Chivallon (2006) who emphasizes that "the diaspora theme has become in itself a rallying center without having clear contours, the notion serving rather to say everything and its opposite" (17). The reality of diaspora communities corresponds to the different experiences of people, to the different types of realities of individuals coming from different geographical places. Each diaspora, like that of Haiti, knows a different journey, a history, a trajectory, a different reality. The reasons individuals leave their country of origin to settle in a foreign land are as diverse as they are varied.

One of the peculiarities of the Haitian radio system is the fact that a very influential component of its audience is outside the border. It is the diaspora that remains very faithful to listening to Haitian radio stations based locally in Haiti and that actively participates in public radio debates. This is a feature of the Haitian radio system that takes on great importance in the context of the digital revolution. It should also be emphasized that the dependence of this part of the public on the Haitian media is a function of their attachment to a Haitian identity. To better analyze the relations of the Haitian public in the diaspora with the media of their country of origin, we introduce into our theoretical framework transnationalism, which is a very flourishing approach in international migration studies. The scientific literature on transnational phenomena of migrants in the context of the development of digital technologies is very recent as we see below. Nevertheless, for some researchers, its theoretical and conceptual depth makes transnationalism a specific and very prosperous field of study. "Many theoretical works have been written, identifying transnationalism as a new and unique area of study. Empirical studies have addressed the theoretical concepts to differing degrees and are still developing methodologies through which to operationalize these concepts" (Bauböck et Faist 2010). Until the end of the twentieth century, much of the attention of researchers interested in migration phenomena was focused on the processes of integration of migrants in their host countries. In fact, they have mainly tried to understand the causes of international migration, while studying integration issues. Several Researchers mobilized the concept of assimilation before making use of the notion of integration (or insertion) which is much rather recent studies on international migration.

The different approaches that preceded transnationalism presented the migrant as a disoriented being, disconnected from the realities of his or her country of origin. Thus, the idea identified in these studies is that the process of integration of migrants resulted in a weakening of the latter's relations with their country of origin. It is as if there is a wall erected between the migrant and his or her country of origin. Nevertheless, the work of other researchers such as (Sayad 1999) has focused on ethnic enclaves and networks woven by migrants. He was interested in both the phenomena of emigration and immigration, which are inseparable yet largely apparent.

CHAPTER 5

Comparative Studies of Hallin and Mancini's Media Systems

Media systems are changing on a global scale. In this chapter, it is a question of presenting, among other things, a synthesis of the work relating to comparative studies of media systems in the world. In recent decades, we have seen an intensification of studies on the transformation of media systems from a comparative perspective (Hallin and Mancini 2004; Von Vorgelegt 2014; De Mooij 2014; Seethaler 2017; Chadwick 2017, and others). In fact, unlike the work of Hallin and Mancini, we do not seek to compare the Haitian radio system with other systems. Rather, it is a diachronic demonstration of the transformation of the Haitian radio system according to three sets of explanatory factors (linguistic, economic and political, and technological) that we will see later in this chapter.

The systems analyzed depend on the socio-cultural, political, and economic conditions or environment in which they operate. Indeed, the studies of Hallin and Mancini (2004) are major references in the field of comparative studies on media systems. The conclusions of their book are based on a field survey of media institutions in eighteen Western countries. They analyze the different characteristics of the media systems of Western countries by establishing links between the different types of media systems analyzed.

Hallin and Mancini's Theoretical Models

As we pointed out at the beginning of this book, the Haitian radio system is made up of a set of actors who are in a position of interdependence. We were particularly interested in these types of relationships. Nevertheless, the idea of a transformation of media systems is not foreign to the work of Hallin and Mancini. This makes their approach useful to us in the study of these transformations. As we will see here, the different models developed by Hallin and Mancini (liberal, polarized pluralist, corporatist) apply only to Western countries. However, the four parameters on which they based their models (market structure, political parallel-ism, professionalization, role of the state) remain relevant to characterizing media systems in Haiti as everywhere in the world. So, we present some fundamen-tal characteristics of the Haitian radio system before presenting the framework for the comparative analysis of Hallin and Mancini's media systems. Hallin and Mancini's conceptual framework starts from four main dimensions from which they characterize and compare the media systems in question.

The first dimension is economic. This is particularly true of the composition of media markets. The second dimension refers to political parallelism, which is explained by the formal or informal relationship between the media and po-litical structures. It also considers the consequences of partisan structures on the management of media regulation systems. The third dimension relates to the degree of professionalization of journalists. It relates to the autonomy of journalists, the way in which professional standards are defined as well as their commitment to the public service. The fourth dimension concerns the role of the State and the legal and regulatory framework governing the action of the media.[1] Hallin and Mancini's approach is part of an analytical perspective based on a systematic comparison of the media in Western democracies in the context of nation states.

Presentation of Hallin and Mancini's Analytical Methods

The conceptual framework developed by Hallin, and Mancini applies only to Western countries that are rich and developed countries. We see that this is not the case for the Haitian media system, which operates in a very particular environment with markedly different characteristics than those of the media systems analyzed. This typology does not apply to the case of Haiti. What in-terests us is the method used by researchers to establish their three types of media systems. So, from this method we can highlight the particularities of the Haitian media system.

The approach and methods used by Hallin and Mancini to characterize West-ern media systems are very useful in achieving our demonstration. They can be

---

1. Note that, according to Patterson (2007), Hallin and Mancini are not the designers of the specified four dimen-sions. Rather, they are the result of the work of Jay Blumler, Colin Seymour-Ure [While Seymour-Ure is listed in the Bibliography, Blumler is not.] and others. He points out that the notion of *political parallelism*, for exam-ple, has its origin in the work of Seymour-Ure (1974) on the political impacts of the means of communication. Nevertheless, he says, Hallin and Mancini go beyond their predecessors in developing the relationships that exist between the different dimensions.

understood as a combination of several dimensions on which their analytical framework is based. The authors particularly seek to determine the relationship between the media and political structures. Hallin and Mancini's comparative analysis of Western media systems is based on an integrative conceptual framework. They compared media systems with similar socio-cultural, political, and economic characteristics. It is a question of determining the points of resemblance and the specific characteristics of media systems according to their compositions and their functioning to arrive at coherent archetypes.

Presentation of Hallin and Mancini's Three Models of Media Systems

The characterization of the systems analyzed by Hallin and Mancini allows them to identify three types of media systems. As we have pointed out, the conceptual framework developed by Hallin and Mancini is structured in four dimensions: the media market, political parallelism, the professionalization of journalism, and the role of the state. The following table presents a synthesis of the three models of the media system of Western countries developed by Hallin and Mancini.

MODEL / PARADIGM	POLARISED PLURALIST	DEMOCRATIC CORPORATIST	LIBERAL
Countries	France • Greece, Italy • Portugal • Spain	Austria • Belgium, Denmark • Finland, Germany • Netherlands • Norway • Sweden • Switzerland	Britain • Canada, Ireland • United States
Newspaper industry	Low newspaper circulation • elite politically oriented press	High newspaper Circulation • early development of mass circulation press	Medium newspaper circulation early • development of mass-circulation commercia press
Political parallelism	High political parallelism • external Pluralism • commentary-oriented journalism • parliamentary or government model Of broadcast governance — politics-over-broadcasting system	External pluralism especially in national press • historically strong party press • shift toward neutral commercial press • politics-in-broadcasting system with substantial autonomy	Neutral commercial Press • information-oriented journalism • internal pluralism (but external in Britain) • professional model of broadcast governance — formally autonomous system

Figure 5. Summary of the three types of media systems
by Hallin and Mancini (2004, p. 67).

The Polarized Model of Pluralism

As summarized in the table above, the Mediterranean or polarized model of pluralism applies to some countries such as Greece, Spain, Portugal, Italy, and France. This is because this model corresponds particularly to countries whose history is marked by the presence of authoritarian political regimes, and which have been slow to take the democratic path. The transition from dictatorship to democracy also leads to strong political parallelism. As a result, this type of political system is characterized by a media space dominated by a politically oriented elite, by a low media diffusion and by a great influence of political and economic forces on media structures (73). Thus, the researchers show a very high rate of parallelism and a strong politicization of the media in the Mediterranean countries while it is lower in other countries studied. They point to a certain ability of journalists to focus on comments rather than facts. There is also a certain media practice in this system of promoting political tendencies. Journalists and the media tend to mobilize their audiences for a political cause. This role of activists is explained by the rather strong links that media owners and journalists maintain with political structures (74). The fact that journalists become politicians or vice versa is a common practice in the Mediterranean system, especially in the case of the Greek media system in which newspapers remain political instruments. This is also the case in the system we are analyzing. Through the results of this study, we see that despite its singularity, the Haitian media system is approaching the Mediterranean model.

The Corporatist Democratic Model

The corporatist democratic model concerns in particular countries in the northern and central regions of Europe. This model is particularly prevalent in countries that have experienced an early development of the media industry and press freedom. It includes countries such as Austria, Finland, Germany, Belgium, Denmark, Norway, and Switzerland. This type of corporatist democratic media system is also characterized by very strong state interventions in the functioning of the media as well as a very coherent culture of freedom of information. Politically linked media and powerful commercial media are doing well, and political parallelism can be seen alongside traditional professional practices dominating journalism. This model is also characterized by a high circulation of newspapers and journalistic practices focused on commentary. There is a high level of formal organization among professional journalists.

The Liberal Model

The third and final type of media system presented by Hallin and Mancini is that of the North Atlantic or the liberal model. It brings together rich Western countries such as the United States, Canada, Ireland, and the United Kingdom. Thus, this grouping shows how media systems are shaped by the cultural and geographical proximity as well as the common historical, economic, and political context of countries. According to the researchers, the media in these countries experienced a high level of development and a high degree of freedom at a very early stage. The liberal model is characterized above all by a dominance of commercial newspapers and a weak political parallelism. It is also marked by a strong professionalization of journalism, but better organized than the media that evolve according to the corporatist democratic model. It is also marked by a limitation of the independence of journalists due to commercial and political pressures on the media.

Here we have just briefly summarized the three models described by Hallin and Mancini. They show some variation in media systems. However, their study also reveals a certain dissimilarity between the proposed models and the degree of transformation of media systems between nation states over time. In the 1970s, the differences between the three groups of media systems characterized through the three models developed by Hallin and Mancini were quite substantial. Nevertheless, a few decades later, at the beginning of the twenty-first century, the differences between the three groups of countries have diminished considerably (251–252). Hallin and Mancini show that the liberal model has become increasingly dominant in both Europe and North America. Nevertheless, they note the existence of certain "counter-tendencies" that tend to limit the spread of the liberal model in other countries.

At the end of their analysis, Hallin and Mancini evoke the thesis of the convergence or homogenization of Western media systems, particularly European, which, according to them, could be pushed toward the liberal model (251). These include European political integration, legislation on the functioning of the media and the demise of traditional mass political parties. They also take into consideration the American influence on the professionalization of journalism and the marketing of European media markets. Their argument is based on observations relating to the process of transformation of Western media systems. They even claim that there is an extension of the process of homogenization or convergence to other parts of the world. If this trend were confirmed and progressed, it could lead to a kind of universalization of the models presented by Hallin and Mancini in the sense that they would be applicable to non-Western countries. However, they point out that this process could also be limited since the elements of the process are rooted in the structural differences between political systems around the world. We see that the convergence thesis is disputed by many researchers because of significant differences found between the systems studied by Hallin and Mancini and the systems of non-Western countries studied by the protesters.

The Weaknesses of Hallin and Mancini's Conceptual Framework

Despite its relevance, theoretical depth, and impact in the scientific community, Hallin and Mancini's (2004) analytical framework is not universal in scope and the authors are aware of this. The dimensions and models that result from their work specifically cover the relationship between the media and the political class in the Western world. The authors do not pretend to extend their typology to all media systems, because there is no homogeneity between media systems. Nevertheless, they consider their conceptual framework to be relevant because it tends to show convergence toward a dominant model, which is the liberal model.

Through their publication, Hallin and Mancini (2017) note a great progress in the comparative analysis of media systems twelve years after the publication of their reference book *Comparing Media Systems* (2004) The researchers point out that "the most significant progress has been made in the development of quantitative indicators of key system-level variables, which permit comparison and exploration of relationship across cases and over time"(Hallin & Mancini 2017,165). The researchers clearly accepted that the field of comparative analysis of media systems has reached a degree of maturity that it did not have at the time of the realization of their original work, fifteen years ago.

Hallin and Mancini recognize the premises and limitations of comparative literature on online media. "The existing comparative literature on online media remains limited, but the beginnings of a research literature in this area are present. Several hypotheses are possible about how internet-based media might relate to existing patterns of variation in media systems" (Hallin and Mancini, 2017, 164). The authors discuss here the possibility of a set of hypotheses about how online media might relate to the patterns of variation that exist in media systems. According to them, one of the likely hypotheses is the fact that online media would be considered a source of convergence. This, according to them, can introduce logic rooted in economic models or universal socio-cultural practices, thus leading to a weakening of the diversities or particularities that exist between nations (Hallin and Mancini, 2017, 164). Indeed, one of the main criticisms of their previous work is the fact that they did not consider the effects of the internet on the media systems studied. Although they are aware of the criticisms addressed to them, they try to justify them by evoking a lack of literature relating to media that are based on the internet.

With this new publication, Hallin and Mancini are revising their initial work based on some of the research published since the publication of their reference work, *Comparing Media System* (2004). This new reading consists in making operational concepts addressed in this work and experimenting with their working environment.

The Halin and Mancini Model: Criticism and Complementarity

Criticisms of Hallin and Mancini's work are numerous. The media system typology they propose has been used to analyze many non-Western media systems. In her doctoral thesis on the Lebanese media system, Vorgelegt Von (2014) tested the validity of the models proposed by Hallin and Mancini (2004). At the end of her empirical analysis, he encourages researchers to conduct new comparative research on non-Western media systems. She concludes that none of Hallin and Mancini's models fit the Lebanese media system. She believes that it is imperative to adapt the dimensions and sub-dimensions defined in the models proposed by Hallin and Mancini for application to other non-Western systems. We have noticed that some researchers like[2] (Boguslawa Dobek-Ostrowska et al. 2010) question a particular type. For example, he questions the very nature of the polarized pluralist model proposed by Hallin and Mancini (2004) which, according to him, is far from universal despite the fact that its characteristics are similar to those of the media systems of some non-Western countries. De

---

2. See chapter 4 of Panier, Wisnique. 2021. «Les transformations du système radiophonique haïtien de 1957 à 2020: Changement et continuité». Québec (Québec): Université Laval.
2file:///Users/wisniquepanier/Downloads/37016-1.pdf.

Mooij (2014) offers an in-depth analysis of the applicability of mass communication theories to non-Western cultures. His work is presented as one of the first attempts at a methodical and accomplished analysis of human and mediatized communication on a global scale. His study is based on a vast corpus of communication theories from all continents. Finally, he questions the assumption that Western theories of human communication and mass communication have universal reach. It shows how culture can have a great influence on personal or mass communicational attitudes in a democratic society.

Indeed, the mass media play a fundamental role in democratic transitions around the world. In the case of Haiti, for example, we see that the media, particularly radio, were used as an instrument in the struggle against the Duvalier dictatorship. In other words, radio has greatly facilitated the transition from dictatorship to democracy in Haiti. Based on the democratic process in certain regions of the world such as Latin America, Africa, and Asia, Voltmer (2013) analyze the interactions that have taken place between political and media transitions. Her study considers the difficulties faced by the media during democratic transitions. It analyzes the legacy or weight of the past on the transformation of emerging media systems. Several themes or some of the dimensions used by Hallin and Mancini to analyze the media systems of Western countries such as media markets, the professionalization of journalists, political parallelism, and the relations between the media and the state are treated in her book.

As we have noticed, researchers use almost the same variables or dimensions as those used by Hallin and Mancini (2004) to analyze the media systems of some non-Western countries. This is also the case for Mushtaq and Baig (2016) who analyze the Indian media system under the comparative model of media and political systems developed by Hallin and Mancini (2004). According to them, the relationship between the media and India's political systems is very complex and requires a greater effort of interpretation. At the end of their work, they conclude that the Indian media system is closer to the liberal model of the North Atlantic countries. They thus consider "clientelism" and "polarized pluralism" as the main characteristics of the Indian political system which leads, they say, to a high "political parallelism" and an "instrumentalization" of the media that are placed in the hands of the political and economic elites.

Through this analysis, we also point out that other research shows that media systems change according to the political, economic, and socio-cultural context of the countries in which they operate. Some researchers such as Seethaler (2017) offer a descriptive analysis of research paradigms and traditions relating to the development and organization of media systems. It sees the latter as a set of interacting media institutions and practices. It describes the structural emergence and transformation of media institutions over time and how they influence both media performance and audience behavior. According to him, studies of media systems highlight two types of approaches. On the one hand, there are normative approaches that are, he says, concealed by the political circumstances of the Cold War period. And on the other hand, there are analytical approaches that have a more recent history. This rather attractive new approach is widely used in current studies. He argues that research on media systems is usually based on previous upheavals in media structures. To this end, it calls into question the potential of the theoretical framework of research related to media systems. According to him, economic development and the multiplication of digital tools are leading to an erasure of boundaries between national markets, media genres, journalistic cultures, audiences, and even between users and producers. This is what we see in the context of the analysis of the transformation of the Haitian radio system.

Some researchers such as Dobek-Ostrowska and Głowacki (2010) show that comparative studies of media systems have been linked to an approach that consists of measuring the media practice of the systems of other countries in relation to the philosophical social foundations of each of the countries in question without taking into account their theoretical foundations and the singularity of their experimental practice in one of his studies. Dobek-Ostrowska (2010) presents a comparative analysis of the reform of the public radio and television system in the United Kingdom and Spain during the years 2004 to 2007. The results of his work show that technological convergence and the propensity for deregulation of the media sector play a fundamental role in the transformation of public broadcasting in the United Kingdom and Spain.

In contrast, other scholars are of the view that media systems are not only embedded in political or economic systems, but are also shaped by cultural values, which are likely to be examined as more invariable than organization. This is in a way what De Mooij (2014) shows in his comparative study of theories and approaches to the analysis of media systems on a global scale. As we have already pointed out, any media system depends on the socio-political, economic, and cultural environment in which it operates. A media system in a democratic country does not function in the same way as one that operates in an authoritarian or dictatorial regime. The case of Haiti, which experienced very ferocious dictatorial periods before entering the democratic era, is a good example. In this sense, Dunn (2014) talks about the creation of a two-tier Russian media system resulting from the reconfiguration of mass media in Russia. In this media system, it shows that most media, especially Russian national television, are strictly controlled, while other types of media such as the internet enjoy greater autonomy. Indeed, it is much more difficult to control the information that circulates on the internet even in the most restrictive societies of freedom of expression.

Through their book, Dobek-Ostrowska and Głowacki (2010, 63–76) analyze Turkey's media system in the light of the three models of Hallin and Mancini. They seek to determine the extent to which the Turkish media system fits into one or other of the three models in question. In fact, the researchers see the latter as a starting point for analyzing how the Turkish media handles news and political actors. Their study aims to determine the way in which politics and political actors are presented to the Turkish people through the main news programs in comparative logic of their performance to that of European countries. In other words, it is a question of determining the European characteristics in the specified emissions. For them, Turkey's possible accession to the European Union remains the most crucial debate underway in the Turkish media. The authors consider the discovery of at least three types of media and political systems within the member states of the European Union as an argument for attesting to the absence of a single "European" media system and a homogeneous and generalized European political system.

It shows that Turkey does not really belong to any of the three media systems in the West. Hence, according to them, there is a need to design an additional model of media system and politics in Eastern or Southern Europe. As we have already pointed out, the grouping carried out by Hallin, and Mancini is profoundly influenced by the geographical, cultural, and political proximity of Western countries. It is in this sense that Dobek-Ostrowska and Głowacki (2010) support the idea that Turkey's geographical location leaves little alternative but to expect a link with the polarized pluralist model. Because, according to them, this is the model that could apply to all the countries of the Mediterranean region and that is essentially suitable for Turkey. To demonstrate this, they address the four main dimensions of the media systems used by Hallin and Mancini (2004) to develop their models.

In a new study on Russian media, Lehtisaari and Miazhevich (2019) present a sketch of different theories relating to Russian media after the fall of the Soviet Union. They particularly seek to determine the extent to which existing media theories can be applied to the Russian context. They present an account of new Russian journalistic practices. At the end of their analysis, they suggest what they call a "wave" evolution of the Russian media. First, they evoke a first wave that is linked to the analysis of what they call the "Glasnost of perestroika," as well as to the disorganization that followed the collapse of the Soviet Union in 1991. Then, there is a wave that was born from a national reflection on the process of the evolution of the Russian media system during the 2000s. And finally, they mention a third wave that is mainly explained by regulatory changes that took place during the 2010s. These regulatory changes are particularly linked to the development of digital technologies and the growing penetration of the internet in Russia, which have major impacts on the functioning of the Russian media system. We see in our case study that digital technologies are the main factor of change in the relations between the actors of the Haitian radio system. This is also a constant in all media systems in the countries of the North as well as those of the South. Digital is omnipresent.

Studies of the Russian media system are numerous. Some researchers like Kiriya (2019) propose a new approach to analyzing what she calls the current duality of the Russian media system, which, according to the author, has been widely examined. Her new approach is to "explain the current Russian media system in terms of institutional conflict between artificially implemented norms and informal rules rooted in the daily practices of market agents and audiences" (Kiriya, 2019, 1). Her study shows that the norms that governed the Russian media system following the fall of the Soviet Union were based on a neoliberal representation that guaranteed the media a certain financial sovereignty over the state. According to the author, the dualistic character of the Russian media system is characterized by the interference of two fundamental elements: on the one hand, the paternalism of the State of informal rules and the tradition of accessibility, as well as the fragmentation of the public sphere.[3]

Other Russian researchers such as Dobek-Ostrowska and Głowacki (2010) present a diagnosis of the conformity of the Russian media system with its political, economic, and ideological model of the time of the Soviet Union. This is the communist, Soviet or Marxist model which, according to the authors, was characterized by state (and party) ownership, centralization, partisan journalism, and (ideological) censorship. On the other hand, they say, there would be a lack of coherence at the level of the post-communist Russian model due to the

---

3. My free translation.

fact that state control still weighs very heavily on the media despite the fact that the latter are increasingly privately owned.[4]

Despite the censorship ban, Russian journalists are forced to write or not write on certain topics considered to be very sensitive that could put the Russian state in a bad position. This means that Russian journalists are not as free as those in Western countries. Through this study, Dobek-Ostrowska and Głowacki (2010) examine in depth the various qualifiers proposed to name the Russian media system as well as the social system in the broad sense. They seek to position the Russian media system in the categorization of media systems developed by Hallin and Mancini (2004). They make use of the four dimensions defined by the latter to distinguish the characteristics of the Russian media system. After a very rich documentation of the Russian case, the authors argue that Russia is often described as an "ideology," "a one-party system," "a center-led economy," "a terrorist police," "a monopoly of communication and a monopoly on arms," or "a monopolistic and total regime." After comparing their conclusions on the Russian media system with three types of media – polarized pluralist, democratic corporatist and liberals – proposed by Hallin and Mancini (2004), they admit that the labels granted to Russia suggest a concordance of the Russian media system with the democratic and liberal model.

The Concept of "Press-Party Parallelism"

The scientific literature shows that other concepts have also been proposed to study media systems. This is the case, for example, of Kempen (2007), which uses the concept of "press-party parallelism" to analyze media systems across fifteen member states of the European Union. This concept differs from political parallelism in that it refers rather to the political participation of citizens.[5] "Moreover, the article investigates the consequences of media-party parallelism for political behavior in a cross-national comparative setting" (Kempen, 2007, 304). The author is particularly interested in the political interests of citizens, the preferences of parties that are treated as dependent variables, and citizens' exposure to the media. It examines the configuration of the public to better analyze the degree of parallelism between the media and political parties. Thus, she studies the relationship between exposure to the media and the political preferences of parties.

---

4. See pages 41–62 of *In Search of a Label for the Russian Media System.*

5. It is not, however, a new concept in the sense that it was used in Seymour-Üre's (1974) work on mass media.

According to Kempen (2007), the concept of media-party parallelism and its possible consequences have been very poorly exploited in comparative studies of media systems. According to her, this concept has remained, until then, at its theoretical stage. There are, she says, four manifestations of media-party parallelism that can be observed both in media content, in the ownership of the news media, in the affiliations of journalists, and about media owners or managers (307). After analyzing the data relating to the 1999 European elections, she manages to demonstrate that media-party parallelism leads to a mobilization of citizens, including those who show a certain lack of interest in politics. "The results showed a considerable degree of variation between countries. In general, the association between newspaper reading and party preferences (press-party parallelism) is stronger than the relationship between TV news viewing and party preferences (television-party parallelism" (Kempen, 2007, 314). The results of her studies show a very significant variation in media-party parallelism between countries and a structuring of the political attitude of European citizens such as their participation in elections.

Toward a Hybrid Model of Media Systems

The development of new digital technologies is disrupting the way media systems operate around the world. It is in this perspective that Chadwick (2017) argues in favor of the concept of a "hybrid media system." He argues the main thesis that political communication is going through a chaotic passage due to the rise of digital media.[6] In addition, other researchers such as Sundaram and Rikakis (2006) speak rather of "experiential media systems" to explain a new complementary model that is developing in the age of digital technologies. This multimedia computing model is developed to interpret and contextualize human activities across time and space. Returning to Chadwick (2017), his book highlights three sets of concepts. This is very enlightening work in the context of digital media development. First, it is a question of the power relations between political actors, media actors, and audiences associated with old and new media (19).

Next, it deals with the notion of the system in the context of digital development. And finally, he addresses the idea of media logic. "The ontology of hybridity constitutes an important and suggestive critique of thinking. I believe

---

6. See Chapter 1, 10.

this ontology provides a fruitful approach to understanding the interactions between older and newer media logic in contemporary politics society and it can
help shed new light on the relative power of actors in a media system" (Chadwick, 2017, 18–19). It was based on the observation of the changing relations
between politicians, the media and the public in Britain and the United States.[7]

These two countries, according to him, have the best characteristics of hybrid media systems (p. 5). It considers the interactions between old and new
media as well as technologies, categories, rules, and attitudes as the basis for
the hybridization of the multimedia system. "We need to understand how newer
media practices in the interpenetrated fields of media and politics adapt and
integrate the logic of older media practices in those fields. We also need to
understand how older media practices in the interpenetrated fields of media
and politics adapt and integrate the logic of newer media practices" (Chadwick,
2017, 5). For him, the key to interpreting the hybrid media system lies in the
fact that it is based on a conceptual understanding of power, but that can be il-
lustrated experimentally. He considers the interference between the old and the
new media to be the origin of the miscegenation of the media system.

Some researchers are particularly interested in the transformation of journalism as a socio-cultural practice. This is the case, for example, for Obijiofor and
Hanusch (2011) who review the different theoretical and practical approaches
to journalism in Western and non-Western cultural contexts.

In their book, they propose keys to understanding the transformation of
journalism practices in different cultural contexts. It shows how media theories
and models evolve over time. Other researchers are more interested in the socio-cultural dimension of the evolution of media systems. This is the case, for
example, of Lee and Chu (1995) who propose a socio-cultural model that, they
say, can be used for intercultural comparison. This proposal is the result of their
study to examine Hong Kong's media system from a socio-cultural perspective.
Their analysis takes into consideration five fundamental factors that characterize a media system. According to the researchers, these are the political structure, the economic structure, the culture of media owners, the culture of media
practitioners, and the culture of the public.

Thus, they determine four media systems that they consider "ideal types"
that come from the combination of the five factors listed. These are: type I, Free
System; type II, relatively free system; type III, relatively repressive system;

---

7. This study is very enlightening for our analysis since we were interested in the change in the relations between
the different actors of the Haitian radio system.

and type IV, repressive system. In conclusion, they point out that the current condition of the media in Hong Kong can be observed as a relatively free system.

However, they say, their observations lead to the fact that the media system in Hong Kong is likely to become a partially repressive system after 1997. Indeed, the various researchers interested in media systems are developing comparative models and procedures to highlight certain common characteristics of media systems in certain countries and their differences according to their geographical context.[8]

As we have just seen, there is a very large body of work in the literature on media systems, particularly Western ones. In our case study, we place particular emphasis on the relationship between journalists and the radio audience. Therefore, we are interested in studies on public participation in radio talk shows. Because journalists and their audience are two fundamental actors in the Haitian radio system. Few researchers have been interested in this aspect.

Studies of public participation in radio broadcasts date back to the 1960s by researchers such as Lerner and Schramm (1967) and Arnstein (1969) (Carpentier 2009). Took up and systematized the forms of citizen participation described by Harry Einstein 1964) by applying them to Belgian community radio. This is about public participation in media debates leading to political decision-making.

His study focuses on the reception of two radio programs in Belgium and on the sustainability of the model of mass communication through new media. The results of its study show that the media broadcast on the internet are far from eliminating the usual forms of participation in traditional media. It notes that participation practices are not unconditionally appreciated by members of the public, and that they are subject to conditions of the possibility rooted in the paradigm of mass communication (Carpentier, 2009, 1).

Some recent studies show that members of the public use digital platforms to participate in radio broadcasts. Through an "analysis of interactions," Ravazzolo (2009) studies the conditions of participation of listeners in the radio debate and finds that "the listeners of 'Interactiv' demonstrate an 'interdiscursive competence' that allows them to speak about and participate effectively in the co-construction of media discourse" (2). For his part, Sandré (2013) was interested in the place of the citizen listener in radio discourse. He analyzes the interview and the debate as two participatory genres. Based on the two pro-

---

8. Further research has probably been done on the post-1997 situation in Hong Kong, but we did not see fit to explore it in this study.

grams: "Interactiv" in the morning and "The Phone Rings" in France Inter, he seeks to determine the mode of operation of the "enunciative device" that leads to the participation of members of the public in the programs studied. In particular, it analyzes the interactive roles of certain actors such as the journalist, the guest and the public participant as well as the place that the media reserve for the latter.

According to the author, "his interactive status replaces that of the moderator of the debate/interviewer by questioning the guests himself and that of the guest by often revealing a position on the subject" (Sandré, 2013, 14). The various contributions of a collective work edited by (Bonini et Monclús 2014)provide an overview of some forms of interaction and emerging contemporary practices between radio and its audience. They are particularly interested in the forms of "content co-creation" that connect producers and listeners based on a variety of cases.

This collective work answers a number of questions relating to the economic and political consequences of the change in the relationship between radio stations and their audience, how the latter is perceived by radio producers in this new radiological landscape, the value of radio audiences in this new framework, the ways in which the public participates in the production of radio content and the way in which the content generated by auditors can be seen as a form of participation. Other researchers propose to analyze the transformations of work practices within newsrooms.

To this end, the research work of the former journalist and university professor, Chantal Francoeur (2012), on "The Transformation of Radio-Canada's Information Service," for which she worked for fifteen years, is very useful to better understand the changes in journalists' working practices in the context of the development of digital tools, in particular the multiplatform work of journalists. Nevertheless, none of these studies seek to understand the impacts of digital technology on the communication contract that connects radio stations and journalists with the public, particularly in the Haitian case.

We put forward the general hypothesis of a transformation of the Haitian radio system, of the relations between the actors under the influence of three series of factors and which lead to a reconfiguration of the system. First, there is a socio-cultural or linguistic factor that essentially translates into the introduction of Creole in radio as a language of communication from the 1970s.

We see that the introduction of Creole in radio has significantly changed the rules of the operation of the radio system. Secondly, there is a factor that is both economic and political, which can be explained by the democratic transition by the transition from dictatorship to democracy since February 6, 1986, which has led to a liberalization of public speech. This factor is also characterized by political instability that leads to moments of recurrent tension within Haitian society. "We have experienced too much political instability in the country. These events undermine each time the foundations of democracy and drag their share of insecurity, misery, and uncertainty,"(Moise 2020), said the President of the Republic of Haiti, Jovenel Moise in his speech of the installation of the members of the new Provisional Electoral Council at the National Palace on September 22, 2020.

We also see that democratization and the political crises that characterize Haitian society are helping to shape the Haitian media system. "For Haitian leaders in recent decades, the retention of power has always taken precedence over democratic strengthening and the establishment of strong independent institutions" (Renois, 2016, 52), which generates constant crises between members of the opposition and the country's political power. And finally, this transformation is explained by the development of digital tools that induce profound changes in the relationships between the different actors. We see how the use of digital tools changes the relationships between the different actors of the system.

Each of these three factors participates in one way or another in the transformation of relations between the different actors that make up the Haitian radio system. Relations between the actors of the Haitian radio system are governed by norms, conventions, and reciprocal expectations that Charron and Le Cam (2012) consider a "public communication contract." The changes in the relations between the actors are above all changes in certain clauses of the contract that connects radio stations, journalists, news sources, advertisers, and state and non-state regulatory bodies that constitute the main actors of the system we analyze. It is from the angle of change in such a communication contract that we apprehend the changes in the relations between the actors.

From all the above, we can deduce that the work of Hallin and Mancini remains a major reference in comparative studies of media systems. Nevertheless, the models proposed by the researchers have limitations that make them not applicable in non-Western countries or less developed countries such as Haiti. Numerous studies carried out in the context of non-Western countries show that the three models presented by Hallin, and Mancini are far from being applicable to the media systems of the countries in question. However, the applied analytical methods of Hallin and Mancini remain fundamental to our demonstration.

No research has yet been done on the Haitian media system. We may believe that some of the observations that are made elsewhere may apply to Haiti, but that country has historical, political, economic, social, and cultural characteristics that lead us to believe that what is observed elsewhere does not necessarily apply in the case of Haiti. Hence the relevance and scientific justification of our study. We have good reason to believe that the Haitian radio system is special compared to the other media systems mentioned above. The importance of our study is justified by the singularity of the Haitian radio system and its potential contribution to the advancement of knowledge on the transformation of media systems, generally in the field of public communication. This is in a way what justifies the proposal of a new theoretical model to analyze media systems like that of Haiti.

CHAPTER 6

The Contribution of the Haitian Case of Studies on Media Systems

We reviewed the different theoretical models proposed by Halin and Mancinni as well as other studies of other non-Western media systems. Considering the specific characteristics of the Haitian media system and its environment, we have concluded that the Haitian media system does not belong to any of the existing models. Our study confirms the limitations of the models developed by Hallin and Mancini. Their conceptual framework is probably ill-adapted to the situation in Haiti.

The Haitian media system has almost nothing in common with the corporatist democratic model that corresponds to the countries of northern and central Europe such as Austria, Finland, Germany, Belgium, Denmark, Norway, and Switzerland. These are the countries that have experienced an early development of the media industry and press freedom. This was not the case for Haiti.

Also, the North Atlantic model or the liberal model does not apply to the Haitian case either. This prototype corresponds to rich Western countries such as the United States, Canada, Ireland, and the United Kingdom. These countries have experienced a very early level of economic growth and freedom. The liberal model is characterized by a preponderance of commercial newspapers, a weak political parallelism, and a strong professionalization of journalism, which is very far from the situation in Haiti.

Among the three models proposed by Hallin and Mancini, the Haitian media system is somewhat like the Mediterranean or polarized system of pluralism because of its strong politicization. Nevertheless, the other elements that characterize the Mediterranean system are absent in the Haitian case. Indeed, the Mediterranean model corresponds to countries such as Greece, Spain, Portugal, Italy, and France, whose history is marked by the presence of despotic political regimes that took the democratic path late. Haiti's entire history is marked by authoritarian regimes. Nevertheless, the democratic transition also leads to

strong political parallelism. The Haitian media system is particularly characterized by a radio space dominated by a politically oriented elite and by a great
influence of political and economic forces on media structures.

The Haitian media system can be compared to the Mediterranean model
due to the strong politicization that characterizes it. The main Haitian radio
programs, especially some editions of news, are tinged with partisan political
commentary. Journalists tend to focus on comments rather than facts. Like the
media system of the countries to which the Mediterranean model applies, there
are certain practices in the Haitian media system that consist in promoting political tendencies or ideologies.

We have also noticed a strong tendency for journalists and the media to mobilize their audiences for certain political causes. Our study shows that many political activists also wear the hat of journalists or hosts of radio talk shows. The
rather strong links between the owners of many media outlets and journalists
with political structures explain this politicization of the Haitian radio system.
Just like in Mediterranean countries, journalists tend to become politicians or
vice versa. This is the case, for example, with the Greek media system in which
newspapers are political instruments (Hallin and Mancini, 2004).

However, while the media systems in the Western countries analyzed by Hallin and Mancini are regulated partly by the market and partly by the state, the
Haitian radio system is regulated only marginally by the state and the market.
Indeed, the Haitian media system is only weakly regulated by market forces,
due to the precariousness of the Haitian media. There is a multiplication of the
number of radio stations in the country, but the advertising market is too small
to support them. In a "normal" market, the big media or media groups would
absorb the smaller ones that don't have the resources to operate. In Haiti, the
increase in the number of stations is explained by political rather than commercial reasons.

In the case of Haiti, although we see some concentration of press ownership, particularly with the Radio Télé Caraïbes group, the advertising market is
too small to encourage media entrepreneurs to buy competitors in the hope of
achieving economies of scale and increasing their share of the advertising market. In fact, the Haitian media system is also fueled by sources of funding other
than advertising, including funds that come from political groups, and whose
distribution does not obey the "normal" laws of the market.

The Haitian media are not financed by the State, at least not officially by
State bodies; the existing legal framework hardly applies. There are almost no

public broadcasting services outside the national radio of Haiti, which has little influence on public opinion. Moreover, due to the precariousness and politicization of the system, radio stations and journalists are poorly autonomous, which translates into a low level of professionalism.

The Model of the Precarious System of Democratic Transition

At the end of our analysis, we conclude that the Haitian media system belongs to a model different from the reference models developed and proposed by Hallin and Mancini (2004) namely: the corporatist democratic model, the Mediterranean or polarized model of pluralism, and the North Atlantic or liberal model. We call this new model: the model of the precarious system of democratic transition. We take into consideration sixteen major parameters to characterize the new model of the media system that we propose. The latter is characterized by a media system dominated by radio, by a strong politicization and therefore a strong political parallelism, by a weak presence of the State in the regulation of the media, by a small market that condemns the media and journalists to precariousness, by a domination of the media space by an elite, through strong diaspora participation in radio and other national debate spaces, and a low level of professionalism.

The environment in which the Haitian media system, which belongs to the model of the precarious system of democratic transition, operates is characterized by recurrent socio-political crises, by a high migration of the population to foreign countries, by a high illiteracy rate, by insecurity, by poverty, by corruption, by the valorization of Creole, by orality, and by the weakness of the country's democratic institutions. These characteristics do not necessarily make Haiti a unique case. Comparative studies could show that such a model applies to other countries, particularly developing countries such as the African countries that are in democratic construction and where radio is the main place of public communication.

Overall Conclusion

The purpose of this study was to analyze the transformations of the Haitian media system over the past sixty years. Nevertheless, we have put the spotlight on radio, which is the dominant media in the country. In this study it is conceived as a "system," a set of actors who are in a relationship of interdependence. We considered that Haitian radio stations and other actors such as the public (local and diaspora), information sources, advertisers, state, and non-state regulatory bodies form a complex system of relations in which each of these actors occupies a certain position and maintains certain relations of interdependence with the other actors. It is essential in this type of interdependence that binds the actors, directly or indirectly, that we have been interested in. We have also considered the fact that this system belongs to an environment composed of other systems (political, economic, cultural) to which it is linked.

The relationships between the different building blocks of the system are examined with the aim of understanding the rules that govern power relations between actors. Indeed, the actors act within a certain framework, according to certain rules or norms, under certain conditions that are imposed on them.

We have not tried to list all the rules that govern the actions of the actors. Instead, we tried to identify the conditions that structure the game in a fundamental way. For example, we see that phenomenon such as the politicization of the system, the valorization of Creole, precariousness, corruption, the low degree of professionalism, and the weakness of the legal framework, we see that all this constitutes, from the point of view of the actors, rules of the game with which they must deal, and which ultimately assign to the actor's places in a power structure. These factors are likely to transform interdependent relationships to the extent that some actors see their dependence increase and their position weaken, while others experience the opposite.

In this study, we were interested in the fact that this system is structured according to power relations, because not all actors in the system are equal in the sharing of power resources and in the exercise of power. In our study, the power structure, which we refer to as a configuration, that is, a set of positions of power that characterize the system. The configuration of this system refers to the state of existing relationships. This is the state of the power or influence relations between the different actors.

We analyzed this system from the point of view of the actors. The latter are conceived as strategic actors who have interests and who act rationally in the defense of their interests. In other words, we consider that people have good reasons to act as they act, and we seek to know these good reasons. We sought to grasp the logic of their behaviors.

This system is a public communication system. As mentioned above, the public debate in Haiti is taking place in a context of transformation of the radio system, due to the use of digital tools by actors. And somewhere, this transformation of the media system changes the conditions for participation in public debates. Thus, the question of public debate is part of our research problem. So, to analyze these exchanges between the actors, we used the concept of public space. However, the particularity of the Haitian public space is that a large part of this public is outside the borders of Haiti. Indeed, the Haitian diaspora actively participates directly and instantaneously in the national political deliberation.

However, this part of the Haitian public has a double belonging because the diaspora also intervenes in another public space, which is that of its host country. So, to analyze the relationships of this component of the public with the Haitian media, we made use of the concept of transnationalism, which is an approach used in the field of international migration studies. This approach allows us to shed light on a specific aspect of our study, which is the participation of the Haitian diaspora in the Haitian public debate. Like other aspects mentioned above, this aspect will be the subject of another more detailed publication.

Also, in a system, the functioning or the game of actors is governed by a set of rules, some of which concern the dynamics of public debates. Therefore, the dynamics of actors in public debates is also analyzed from the perspective of the metaphor of the public communication contract. This concept allows us to consider certain rules relating to public communication. All the rules and mutual expectations that govern the relations between the communication partners. This concept allowed us to analyze the changes in the rules of the game and the power relations between the different actors of the Haitian radio system.

In summary, this book allows us to highlight several limitations, perspectives, and necessary deepening of certain aspects mentioned that deserve to be developed. Otherwise, this book gives a global idea of the Haitian media system, and the next works that will complete it. Specific works on the promotion of Creole as a language of public communication in radio, the politicization of the Haitian media system, the impact of digital technology on the functioning of the Haitian media system, radio debate programs, and the participation of the Haitian diaspora in national political deliberation will complete the work begun in this book.

The interest of our study from which this book derives is that it has several limitations, at the same time as it suggests new avenues of research. One of the biggest difficulties we have encountered is the lack of available documentary data on the evolution of the Haitian media to corroborate some interview and observation data. This made our diachronic approach difficult. Any work to document the situation of the media in Haiti would be welcome. Nevertheless, we were able to collect several clues that allowed us to establish certain facts or to support certain statements of our respondents.

One of the contributions of our study to the advancement of knowledge is to show how the relationships between the main actors of the Haitian radio system have changed under the influence of three sets of factors, but without reconfiguring the entire system. Also, this study is in a way a clearing work that has allowed us to raise several new questions for which there are no answers yet in the scientific literature. The greatest contribution of this book is the proposal of a new theoretical framework for analyzing non-Western media systems according to a set of parameters.

As a result, this book can be considered as the beginning of a research program on the Haitian media system that has so far not been studied. The particularity of the socio-economic and political conditions in which the Haitian media system evolves is a particular object of study and conducive to advancing knowledge in the field of public communication in general.

It would be important to carry out a more systematic study of the content of public debates in Haiti. A quantitative analysis of the content of the radio debate programs would allow us to better understand the different themes that are debated through these programs, to better profile the participants, to understand the dynamics of the forces involved, the criteria for selecting the participants as well as the importance given to issues related to politics in relation to other social subjects, economic and cultural. To achieve this, this radio content will have to be supplemented by interviews with journalists and news sources. Also, to understand people's motivation to participate in talk radio programs, a survey of listeners would also be necessary.

Since 1986, Haiti has begun an endless democratic transition, and Haitians are increasingly motivated to participate in radio talk shows. It would be important to investigate the difficulties faced by communication partners and the strategies put in place by marginal groups to try to participate in public debates through qualitative surveys of these groups. Much more systematic quantitative analyses of public debate programs will have to be carried out. This will make it possible to better identify the themes that are addressed in the programs. This is also the case for information reported in news editions. Such analyses will make it possible to better understand the issues through the protagonists staged. These new lines of research are among the priorities of researchers at the Center for Interdisciplinary Studies on Haitian Media (CEIMH).

POSTFACE

At the beginning of her research work, Wisnique Panier was interested in the impact of digital technologies on radio in Haiti. But soon he was led to broaden the perspective. It seemed too simplistic to try to describe and explain a possible transformation of the Haitian radio system by considering only the technological dimension; rather, it was necessary to observe the evolution of radio in a broader context, that of the transformation of Haitian society.

In addition to technology, two conditions seemed decisive in the transformation of Haitian society and, consequently, of Haitian radio: the valorization of Creole as a language of public communication and the fall of the Duvalier regime and what will follow, that is to say a long and laborious undertaking of building democratic institutions.

From there, it was easy to convince oneself that the combination of technological changes, the valorization of Creole and the fall of the dictatorship created a new context that was likely to profoundly change the functioning of radio in Haiti and the relationship that people have with it. The French-speaking elite would no longer be the only group to be heard on the airwaves; its domination would be weakened; the people would be heard. Radio would no longer be under the yoke of political power. With digital technology, the conditions for the production and circulation of information would no longer be the same; access to information would be facilitated; radio would establish new relations with the population. In short, there was going to be, what the author calls a "reconfiguration of the Haitian radio system"; the fundamental characteristics of the system were going to be unrecognizable.

However, it turns out that the observations made by the researcher do not confirm the hypothesis. And that's what makes this research so interesting. Wisnique Panier's analyses show that technological change does not occur in a cultural, social, and political vacuum. And we see during his analysis how change is modulated and partly hindered by and through social structures and power relations that profoundly characterize Haitian society.

What this research shows is not that these factors have been without effect on radio in Haiti. The author insists that the changes are significant. The valorization of Creole is not trivial in the history of Haiti. It will even contribute to the fall of the Duvalier regime. However, speaking Creole on the radio did not prevent the French-speaking elite from maintaining its position of domination. After the fall of Duvalier Jr., radio was no longer under the control of the dictatorship, but it remained politicized, polarized and instrumentalized by political forces. After Duvalier there was established what Hallin, and Mancini (quoted by the author) call a strong "political parallelism" which meant that radio did not develop as an autonomous institution in relation to political forces.

The changes are not trivial, but they have not led to structural upheavals. This is so because, according to the thesis put forward by the author, the radio system in Haiti, in its nature and functioning, is defined by economic, social, and political factors that have a structural and historical character and that represent a considerable force of inertia. The changes are real and significant, but they have not affected the power structure in the radio system. The same categories of actors occupy the same positions of power and the logic that prevail in the system remain, for the most part, unchanged. The Francophone cultural elite, which is dominant economically, politically, and culturally, has not changed. Even divided politically, it maintains its grip on the radio, following modalities (politicization, corruption) and under conditions (recurrent political crises, poverty, illiteracy, insecurity, dependence on international aid) that remained the same after the fall of Duvalier.

Wisnique Panier's work takes on prominence in media studies for at least two reasons. First, it advances knowledge about a case that of Haiti, which is very poorly documented. And this is a difficult case to study. Haiti does not find all the contextual and factual data that is easily found in rich countries: for example, data on the financing and profitability of radio, on advertisers' advertising expenses, on the composition and behavior of audiences, on the socio-economic profile of the population of journalists, on their professional values, etc. I can testify that Mr. Panier spared no effort to find the information he needed, but we must admit that he worked in a context where access to information is very difficult.

Second, Wisnique Panier's work brings constructive criticism to the theory of media systems developed by Hallin and Mancini, who are authoritative on the subject. The model of the precarious system of democratic transition proposed by the author deserves the attention of researchers because it makes it possible to characterize media systems in different countries that escape the typology proposed by Hallin and Mancini. Admittedly, as the author points out, the Haitian system is, in some respects, related to the Mediterranean model theorized by Hallin and Mancini and which corresponds to countries such as Greece, Spain, Portugal, Italy and France. But it is still a distant kinship. Haitian society has more common points with other countries, particularly in Africa, than with these European countries: it is a developing country, whose population is poor and poorly educated, dominated politically and culturally by an educated elite, it is a country in democratic construction, strongly polarized and which is experiencing successive political crises. in which public communication is focused on orality and therefore on radio. Media theories are most often designed by researchers in developed countries so that they are often unable to account for what is happening in developing countries. Hence the importance of contributions such as that of Wisnique Panier.

The author knows Haitian radio well, having worked there as a journalist. This status as a former journalist offered him the great advantage of knowing the environment he wanted to study, but also posed a huge challenge: this knowledge of the environment can be largely tinged (not to say contaminated) by a system of professional values shared by journalists, which leads the journalist-turned-researcher to make moral judgments bascd on these values. Wisnique Panier therefore had to distance himself from a habitus of a professional journalist to adopt that of the researcher. To a journalistic conception of journalism and radio, it was necessary substitute a scientific theory and method. A conversion that is not self-evident and that Wisnique Panier has done very well. Journalist Panier turned researchers did not question whether the people who work on radio in Haiti are doing their job well or not, whether their behavior is moral or not, or whether he would have acted differently than they did. Rather, he considered that what he studied was a system of relations, a framework of action in which the actions of an actor are explained by the nature of the relations he has with the other actors of the system. This systemic (or relational) conception is coupled with a strategic approach which, basically, consists in saying that the actors act rationally, that they act in the best way, from their point of view, and according to their interests. The researcher is therefore led to wonder what is the logic of their actions, why and how it is a good idea, from their point of view, to act as they act. It is not in moral judgment; it seeks to understand (in the Weberian sense) the behavior of the actors to explain the dynamics of the system of relations.

Wisnique Panier was able to address sensitive subjects, in this case issues relating to corruption, the ethics of radio and political professionals, political polarization, but without falling into trial, condemnation, blame. He explains to us the situation of the actors of the radio, he makes us understand, without judging him and without bringing the reader to judge him. His work as a researcher stops where moral judgment begins, and that's fine.

Jean Charron
Université Laval
Québec

BIBLIOGRAPHY

Altéma, Jean-Marie. 2016. «Le CONATEL présente l'état des lieux du service de la radiodiffusion sonore en Haïti». *CONATEL*, 2 septembre 2016. http://www.conatel.gouv.ht/node/242.

Bartholomew, Sulivan. 2011. «The New Age of Radio How ITCs Are Changing Rural Radio in Africa». http://farmradio.wpengine.netdna-cdn.com/wp-content/uploads/farmradio-ictreport2011.pdf.

Bastien, Sonny, et David Hartt. 1980. *Histoire de la radiodiffusion en Haiti: Pasteur David Hartt*. Audio. Port-au-Prince. https://repository.duke.edu/dc/radiohaiti/RL10059-RR-0202_01.

Baubock, Rainer, et Thomas Faist, éd. 2010. *Diaspora and transnationalism: concepts, theories and methods*. Amsterdam: Amsterdam University Press. «Baubock2010 1..357 - Diaspora_and_Transnationalism.pdf». s. d. Consulté le 8 février 2016. http://cadmus.eui.eu/bitstream/handle/1814/14318/Diaspora_and_Transnationalism.pdf.

Bonaparte, Michel. 1995. «Haiti, du l'art du griot aujourd'hui». At *À la recherche de nouvelles approches en matière de journalisme et de développement international = Searching for new directions in journalism and development*, The graduate school of journalism, 114-16. Québec.

Bonini, Tiziano, et Belén Monclús. 2014. *Radio Audiences and Participation in the Age of Network Society*. Routledge.

Bourdieu, Pierre. 2012. *La distinction critique sociale du jugement*. Paris: Editions de Minuit: Maison des sciences de l'homme. http://banq.pretnumerique.ca/accueil/isbn/9782707337214.

Brin, Colette, Jean Charron, et Jean de Bonville, éd. 2004. *Nature et transformation du journalisme: théorie et recherches empiriques*. Québec: Les Presses de l'Université Laval.

Brin, Colette, Jean Charron, et Jean De Bonville. 2004. «Le journalisme et le marché: De la concurrence à l'hyperconcurrence». At *Nature et transformation du journalisme: Théorie et recherches empiriques*, PUL, 454. Québec.

Bruneau, Michel. 2004. *Diasporas et espaces transnationaux*. Collection Villes-géographie. Paris: Anthropos : Diffusion Economica.

Campbell, Elaine. 2013. «Public Sphere as Assemblage: The Cultural Politics of Roadside Memorialization: Public Sphere as Assemblage». *The British Journal of Sociology* 64 (3): 526-47. https://doi.org/10.1111/1468-4446.12030.

Carpentier, Nico. 2009. «Participation Is Not Enough: The Conditions of Possibility of Mediated Participatory Practices». *European Journal of Communication*, november. https://doi.org/10.1177/0267323109345682.

Castells, Manuel. 2009. *The Rise of the Network Society: The Information Age: Economy, Society, and Culture Volume I*. 2nd edition. Chichester, West

Sussex ; Malden, MA: Wiley-Blackwell.

Chadwick, Andrew. 2017. *The Hybrid Media System: Politics and Power*. Oxford University Press.

Chandessais, Charles A. 1994. *Introduction à l'étude des systèmes (notions de base)*. Éditions scientifiques et Psychotechniques. France: EAP.

Charaudeau, Patrick. 1993. «Le contrat de communication dans la situation classe». in *Inter-Actions, J.F.Université de Metz*, 9. http://www.patrick-charaudeau.com/Le-contrat-de-communication-dans.html.

———. 1997. *Le discours d'information médiatique: la construction du miroir social*. Collection Médias-recherches. Paris : Paris: Nathan ; Institut national de l'audiovisuel.

———. 2006. «Discours journalistique et positionnements énonciatifs. Frontières et dérives». *Semen. Revue de sémio-linguistique des textes et discours*, no 22 (novembre). http://journals.openedition.org/semen/2793.

———. 2011. *Les médias et l'information. L'impossible transparence du discours*. Vol. 2e éd. Médias-Recherches. Louvain-la-Neuve: De Boeck Supérieur. https://www.cairn.info/les-medias-et-l-information--9782804166113.htm.

Charaudeau, Patrick, Dominique Maingueneau, et Jean-Michel Adam. 2002. *Dictionnaire d'analyse du discours*. Paris: Seuil.

Charron, Jean. 1990. «La production de l'actualité politique: Une analyse stratégique des relations entre la presse parlementaire et les autorités politiques». Québec: UNIVERSITÉ LAVAL (département des sciences politiques faculté des sciences sociales).

———. 2014. *Du journalisme d'information au journalisme de communication*. Vidéo. Conférence du séminaire 2014 de la Chaire pour le développement de la recherche sur la culture d'expression française en Amérique du Nord (CEFAN). canada. https://www.youtube.com/watch?v=gfXOcluMQuA&t=4482s.

———. 2016. «Le journalisme en tant que dispositif de médiation dans la communication publique». *Inédit*.

Charron, Jean, et Jean de Bonville. 2002. *Le journalisme dans le système médiatique: concepts fondamentaux pour l'analyse d'une pratique discursive*. Québec: Département d'information et de communication, Université Laval.

Charron, Jean, et Jean De Bonville. 2002. «Le journalisme dans le 'système' médiatique Concepts fondamentaux pour l'analyse d'une pratique discursive». *Études de communication publique*, no 16: 57. http://www.com.ulaval.ca/fileadmin/contenu/docs_pdf/articles/etudes_com_publ/16ecp.pdf.

Charron, Jean, et Florence Le Cam. 2018. «Médias, institutions et espace public : le contrat de communication publique». *Les Études de communication publique*, no Cahier numéro 21: 238. http://www.cem.ulaval.ca/pdf/ECP21_Brouillon_Contrat_comm.pdf.

Chiara, Liguori. 2016. «Haïti, nous avons un problème...». At *Amnistie internationale*. http://www.amnistie.ca/sinformer/communiques/international/2016/haiti/haiti-nous-avons-un-probleme.

Chivallon, Christine. 2006. «Diaspora: ferveur académique autour d'un mot». https://halshs.archives-ouvertes.fr/halshs-00170065.

Crozier, Michel, et Erhard Friedberg. 1977. *L'acteur et le système: les contraintes de l'action collective.* Paris: Éditions du Seuil.

———. 2014. *L'acteur et le système les contraintes de l'action collective.* Paris: Éd. du Seuil.

Crozier, Michel, et Jean-Claude Thoenig. 1975. «La régulation des systèmes organisés complexes: Le cas du système de décision politico-administratif local en France». *Revue Française de Sociologie* 16 (1): 3. https://doi.org/10.2307/3321128.

Dagmar. 2012. «HAITIMedia and Telecoms Landscape Guide». *Infoasaid.* http://www.cdacnetwork.org/contentAsset/raw-data/c631e13a-83b4-4c7c-8a2a-6a364036398d/attachedFile.

Dahlberg, Lincoln. 2001. «The Internet and Democratic Discourse: Exploring The Prospects of Online Deliberative Forums Extending the Public Sphere». *Information, Communication & Society* 4 (4): 615-33. https://doi.org/10.1080/13691180110097030.

Dahlgren, Peter. 2015. «The Global Public Sphere: Public Communication in the Age of Reflective Interdependence». *Information, Communication & Society* 18 (12): 1423-25. https://doi.org/10.1080/1369118X.2015.1020824.

Dahlgren, Peter, Marc Abélès, Daniel Dayan, et Éric Maigret. 1994. «L'Espace public et les médias». *Hermès, La Revue N°* 13-14 (1): 243-62. http://www.cairn.info/resume.php?ID_ARTICLE=HERM_013_0243.

Dahlgren, Peter, et Marc Rilieu. 2000. «L'espace public et l'internet. Structure, espace et communication». At *Réseaux, Communiquer à l'ère des réseaux,* 18 (100): 157-86. https://doi.org/10.3406/reso.2000.2217.

De Mooij, Marieke. 2014. *Human and Mediated Communication around the World a Comprehensive Review and Analysis.* Cham: Springer International Publishing.

Desquiron, Jean. 1997. «L'Histoire de la presse en Haiti». At *Les journalistes parlent...,* Édition La Ruche, 1-6. Port-au-Prince.

Dobek-Ostrowska, Bogusława. 2010. *Comparative Media Systems: European and Global Perspectives.* Budapest; New York: Central European University Press. http://site.ebrary.com/id/10425234.

Dobek-Ostrowska, Bogusława, and Michał Głowacki. 2010. *Comparative Media Systems: European and Global Perspectives.* Central European University Press. https://muse.jhu.edu/book/16039.

Dobek-Ostrowska, Boguslawa, Michał Głowacki, Karol Jakubowicz, and Miklós Sükösd. 2010. *Comparative Media Systems: European and Global Perspectives.* Central European University Press.

Donati, Pierpaolo. 2004. «La relation comme objet spécifique de la sociologie». *Revue du MAUSS* no 24 (2): 233-54. https://doi.org/10.3917/rdm.024.0233.

Dunn, John A. 2014. «Lottizzazione Russian Style: Russia's Two-tier Media System». *Europe-Asia Studies* 66 (9): 1425-51. https://doi.org/10.1080/09668136.2014.956441.

Duval, Frantz. 2016. «Pourra-t-on arrêter à temps le dysfonctionnement général des institutions haïtiennes?» *Le Nouvelliste*, 20 August 2016. http://

lenouvelliste.com/lenouvelliste/article/161181/Pourra-t-on-arreter-a-temps-le-dysfonctionnement-general-des-institutions-haitiennes.

Duvalier, François. 1969. «Décrêt-Loi créant le Conatel». *LE MONITEUR JOURNAL OFFICIEL DE LA REPUBLIQUE D'HAITI.* http://www.conatel. gouv.ht/sites/default/files/DecretCreationCONATEL27Septembre1969.pdf.

Francoeur, Chantal. 2012. *La transformation du service de l'information de Radio-Canada.* Québec: Presses de l'Université du Québec.

Fraser, Nancy. 2005. «La transnationalisation de la sphère publique». March 2005. http://www.republicart.net/disc/publicum/fraser01_fr.htm.

Habermas, Jürgen. 1988. *L'espace public: archéologie de la publicité comme dimension constitutive de la société bourgeoise.* Critique de la politique Payot. Paris: Payot.

«Haïti - FLASH: Haïti 3e pire pays au monde en terme d'accès à l'électricité - HaitiLibre.com: Toutes les nouvelles d'Haiti 7/7». 2017. www.haitilibre. com. HaitiLibre.com. 2017. https://www.haitilibre.com/article-23305-haiti-flash-haiti-3e-pire-pays-au-monde-en-terme-d-acces-a-l-electricite.html.

Hallin, Daniel C., and Paolo Mancini. 2004. *Comparing media systems: three models of media and politics.* Communication, society, and politics. Cambridge ; New York: Cambridge University Press.

———. 2017. «Ten Years After Comparing Media Systems : What Have We Learned?» *Political Communication* 34 (2): 155-71. https://doi.org/10.108 0/10584609.2016.1233158.

Huntington, Samuel P. 1997. *Le choc des civilisations.* Paris: O. Jacob.

Jean-Paul, Jacklin. 2022. «Haïti 100 ans de radiodiffusion». Livre. Paris.

Kastoryano, Riva. 2013. «Le nationalisme transnational turc ou la redéfinition du nationalisme par les 'Turcs de l'extérieur'». At *Nationalismes en mutation en Méditerranée orientale,* édité par Alain Dieckhoff, 249-66. Histoire. Paris: CNRS Éditions. http://books.openedition.org/editionscnrs/2410.

Kempen, Hetty van. 2007. «Media-Party Parallelism and Its Effects: A Cross-National Comparative Study». *Political Communication* 24 (3): 303-20. https://doi.org/10.1080/10584600701471674.

Kiriya, Ilya. 2019. «New and old institutions within the Russian media system». *Russian Journal of Communication* 11 (1): 6-21. https://doi.org/10.1080 /19409419.2019.1569551.

«La participation aux radios communautaires bèlges». 1964. https://www. otrcat.com/p/harry-einstein.

Lancien, Thierry. 2005. «Du 'temps de cerveau humain disponible'». *La revue Toudi, no Toudi mensuel #69.* https://www.larevuetoudi.org/fr/story/du-temps-de-cerveau-humain-disponible.

Lee, Paul S. N., and Leonard L. Chu. 1995. «Hong Kong media system in transition: A socio-cultural analysis». *Asian Journal of Communication* 5 (2): 90-107. https://doi.org/10.1080/01292989509364725.

Lehtisaari, Katja, et Galina Miazhevich. 2019. «Introduction: The Russian Media System at a Crossroads». *Russian Journal of Communication* 11 (1): 1-5. https://doi.org/10.1080/19409419.2019.1567378.

Leterre, Thierry. 2010. «L'Internet: espace public et enjeux de connaissance». *Cahiers Sens public*, no 7-8 (January): 203-17. http://www.cairn.info/resume.php?ID_ARTICLE=CSP_007_0203.

Mabi, Clément, and Anaïs Théviot. 2014. *S'engager sur Internet: mobilisations et pratiques politiques*. Grenoble: Presses Universitaires de Grenoble.

Margolis, Michael, and David Resnick. 2000. *Politics as Usual: The Cyberspace «Revolution»*. Sage Publications.

Mathien, Michel. 1989. *Le système médiatique: le journal dans son environnement*. Langue, linguistique, communication. Paris: Hachette.

————. 1992. *Les journalistes et le système médiatique*. Hachette Université Langue linguistique communication. Paris: Hachette.

Mhagama, Peter. 2015. «Radio Listening Clubs in Malawi as Alternative Public Spheres». *Radio Journal: International Studies in Broadcast & Audio Media* 13 (1): 105-20. https://doi.org/10.1386/rjao.13.1-2.105_1.

Miège, Bernard. 2010. *L'espace public contemporain approche info-communicationnelle*. Grenoble: Presses universitaires de Grenoble.

Ministère de l'information et de la Communication. 1986. « Un siècle de législation sur la presse et de la communication en Haïti 1885-1985 ». MCC.

Moïse, Claude. 2013. «La presse haitienne en diaspora: Situation et responsabilités». *Conjonction: La revue franco-haitienne de l'Institut français en Haiti Presse en Haiti: Passé et présent* (225): 13-18.

Moise, Jovenel. 2020. «Élections: le CEP du 22 septembre». Port-au-Prince, Haïti, septembre 22. https://lenouvelliste.com/article/221253/elections-le-cep-du-22-septembre.

Mucchielli, Alex. 2004. «Recherche qualitative et production de savoirs». Actes du colloque *RECHERCHE QUALITATIVE ET PRODUCTION DE SAVOIRS*, no 1: 34. http://www.recherche-qualitative.qc.ca/documents/files/revue/hors_serie/hors_serie/texte%20Muchielli%20actes.pdf.

Mushtaq, Sehrish, and Dr. Fawad Baig. 2016. «Indian Media System: An Application of Comparative Media Approach». *South Asian Studies* 31 (December): 45-63.

Obijiofor, Levi, and Folker Hanusch. 2011. *Journalism Across Cultures: An Introduction*. Macmillan International Higher Education.

Parham, Angel Adams. 2005. «Internet, Place, and Public Sphere in Diaspora Communities». *Diaspora: A Journal of Transnational Studies* 14 (2): 349-80. https://doi.org/10.1353/dsp.0.0020.

Patterson, Thomas E. 2007. «Comparing Media Systems: Three Models of Media and Politics , by Daniel C. Hallin and Paolo Mancini: Cambridge, England: Cambridge University Press, 2004. 358 Pp. $75.00 Cloth, 29.99 Paper». *Political Communication* 24 (3): 329-31. https://doi.org/10.1080/10584600701471708.

Pierre Étienne, Sauveur. 2007. *L'énigme haitienne: Échec de l'État moderne en Haiti*. PUM. Montreal, [Québec: Les Presses de l'Université de Montréal.

Pierre Louis, Luné Roc. 2011. *Communication et espace public. Une reconstruction à travers l'espace public politique haïtien*. Louvain-La-Neuve: Presses Universitaires.

Pierre, Serge Philippe. 2014. «La Communication Gouvernementale En

Haïti: Le Cas de PetroCaribe». Thèse ou essai doctoral accepté, Montréal (Québec, Canada): Université du Québec à Montréal. http://www.archipel.uqam.ca/6433/.

Rasmussen, Terje. 2014. «Internet and the Political Public Sphere». *Sociology Compass* 8 (12): 1315-29. https://doi.org/10.1111/soc4.12228.

Ravazzolo, Elisa. 2009. «Modalité de participation au dialogue dans une émission radiophonique interactive». Text. http://www.revue-signes.info. 30 July 2009. http://www.revue-signes.info/document.php?id=1181.

Renois, Clarens. 2016. *Sortir Haïti du chaos*. C3 Éditions. Port-au-Prince.

Rioux, Sébastien, and Frédérick Guillaume Dufour. 2008. «La sociologie historique de la théorie des relations sociales de propriété». Actuel Marx, no 43 (août): 126-39. https://doi.org/10.3917/amx.043.0126.

Roc Pierre Louis, Luné. 2020. «Les médias haïtiens dans la crise du coronavirus ou l'épreuve du trilemme de Münchhausen (1ère partie)». *Les Carnets Nord/Sud* (blog). 17 April 2020. https://lescarnetsnordsud.blog/2020/04/17/lune-roc-pierre-louis-les-medias-haitiens-dans-la-crise-du-coronavirus-1/.

Sandré, Marion. 2013. «Quelle place pour le citoyen-auditeur dans le discours radiophonique ? Analyse de genres participatifs». *Cahiers de praxématique*, no 61 (December). http://journals.openedition.org/praxematique/1932.

Sayad, Abdelmalek. 1999. *La double absence: des illusions de l'émigré aux souffrances de l'immigré*. Collection Liber. Paris: Seuil.

Seethaler, Josef. 2017. *Media Systems Theory*. Oxford University Press. https://doi.org/10.1093/obo/9780199756841-0185.

Seymour-Üre, Colin. 1974. *The political impact of mass media. Communication & society*. London, Beverly Hills, Calif: Constable; Sage Publications.

Sundaram, Hari, and Thanassis Rikakis. 2006. «Experiential Media Systems». At *Encyclopedia of Multimedia*, édité par Borko Furht, 225-33. Boston, MA: Springer US. https://doi.org/10.1007/0-387-30038-4_73.

UNESCO. 2019. «Statistiques sur la radio». UNESCO. http://www.unesco.org/new/fr/unesco/events/prizes-and-celebrations/celebrations/international-days/world-radio-day-2013/statistics-on-radio/.

Unicef. 2017. «Statistiques | Haïti | UNICEF». Unicef. 2017. https://www.unicef.org/french/infobycountry/haiti_statistics.html.

Van Den Bos, Matthijs, and Liza Nell. 2006. «Territorial Bounds to Virtual Space: Transnational Online and Offline Networks of Iranian and Turkish–Kurdish Immigrants in the Netherlands». *Global Networks* 6 (2): 201-20. https://doi.org/10.1111/j.1471-0374.2006.00141.x.

Voltmer, Katrin. 2013. *The media in transitional democracies. Contemporary political communication*. Cambridge: Polity.

von, Sarah El Richani vorgelegt. 2014. «Comparative Readings of the Lebanese Media System». Thesis, Germany: Philosophischen Fakultät der Universität Erfurt. https://www.db-thueringen.de/servlets/MCRFileNodeServlet/dbt_derivate_00033062/Dissertation_El_Richani_Sarah.pdf.

Wikipédia. 2020. «Numérique». At *Wikipedia*. https://fr.wikipedia.org/w/index.php?title=Num%C3%A9rique&oldid=171706617.

www.ingramcontent.com/pod-product-compliance
Lightning Source LLC
Chambersburg PA
CBHW041935260326
41914CB00010B/1306